Provocative Syntax

Linguistic Inquiry Monographs
Samuel Jay Keyser, general editor

A complete list of books published in the Linguistic Inquiry Monographs series appears at the back of this book.

Provocative Syntax

Phil Branigan

The MIT Press
Cambridge, Massachusetts
London, England

Series Foreword

We are pleased to present the sixty-first in the series *Linguistic Inquiry Monographs*. These monographs present new and original research beyond the scope of the article. We hope they will benefit our field by bringing to it perspectives that will stimulate further research and insight.

Originally published in limited edition, the *Linguistic Inquiry Monographs* are now more widely available. This change is due to the great interest engendered by the series and by the needs of a growing readership. The editors thank the readers for their support and welcome suggestions about future directions for the series.

Samuel Jay Keyser
for the Editorial Board

1 Introduction

The central concern of this study is syntactic movement, and more precisely, the forces that drive such movement. Chomsky's (1975, 1957) analyses showed that no description of natural language syntax will be adequate unless it includes some notion of movement operations in a syntactic derivation. With the degree of understanding we have managed approximately fifty years later, it now seems likely that such movement transformations are formally simple operations, in which a single phrase is displaced from its original position within a phrase marker, frequently to appear at the "edge" of the same phrase marker. But the mechanics of this simple operation are still murky and controversial.

The problematic aspects of minimalist movement theory have been discussed elsewhere in the literature. (See Lasnik 2003, Roberts and Roussou 1998, and Zwart 2001, among many, for discussion.) What follows is simply a quick summary of the central issues that motivate this study.

In recent versions of minimalist syntactic theory, movement is driven by an "EPP feature" borne by a head that identifies a goal with which to agree. For example, in the derivation of (1), T agrees with *the message*.

(1) The message was transmitted.

What is more, T has an EPP feature that requires that it acquire a specifier. The phrase with which it agrees is automatically selected to fulfill this function, and remerges at the TP root. Similarly, in (2), C bears an EPP feature that is satisfied because when C agrees with the *wh*-feature of *when*, the *wh*-phrase remerges at the CP root to become its new specifier.

(2) When should our people call?

Thus movement is made possible by the prior agreement relation, but it actually occurs only when the agreeing head demands a specifier.

If we look more closely at this movement theory, we can isolate what is crucial. There are two separate components to movement in this approach. One is the probe-goal relation that enables agreement. The other is the EPP feature.

Probes are syntactic heads with one or more unvalued features. Goals are syntactic objects in the c-command domain of a probe that carry features that can supply the missing values to the probe. So the goal in (1) supplies the value for ϕ-features on T; the goal in (2), values for the *wh*-feature on C.

The EPP feature is a development of the earlier "Extended Projection Principle," the function of which was to ensure that sentences have subjects. Historically in generative theory, the observation that sentences need subjects becomes one with substantial theoretical import only after the adoption of Stowell's (1981) project to eliminate phrase structure rules from syntax. If one's model of grammar includes phrase structure rules, then a rule like S → NP VP—or even TP → nP T'—can be used to ensure the presence of a subject. If such rules do not exist, then some other means must be found.

The original EPP consisted of the Projection Principle plus a statement that sentences require specifiers. (According to Chomsky (1982, 10), "We may think of [the EPP] as a general principle governing D-structures, hence also governing structures derived from them.")

The EPP was an ad hoc principle, and subsequent incarnations have not improved on its status, but it remains indispensable in some form or other simply because it remains true that sentences must have subjects, in English and many other languages.[1] Minimalist analyses have typically been explicit on this point, and the "EPP feature" is currently understood to be an irreducible (possibly parameterized) property of T, and of other heads that happen to be associated with the landing site for phrasal movement.[2]

However, even if we have to grant that the EPP in some form is a primitive of the grammar, we may still prod away at how this concept achieves its purpose. It is clear that any syntactic "rule" must be either representational or derivational. This is as true of the EPP as of any other condition on grammatical acceptability. The original EPP was formulated as a representational principle to be satisfied at D-structure. Lacking any concept equivalent to D-structure, we cannot expect to maintain a rule of this sort in our model of grammar. It can still be asked if the EPP could be taken to be a rule applying at one of the interface levels of representation—that is, at PF or LF.

It is clear that there can be no PF requirement that a given category have a specifier, since specifiers are often invisible. To take two quick examples, consider the phonetically empty specifier for embedded TP in (3a) and the silent operator in [Spec, C] of the relative clause in (3b).

(3) a. The wolf seems [$_{TP}$ t to have eaten Red Riding Hood].
   b. the wolf [$_{CP}$ OP that we chased t]

And there cannot be an LF constraint to this effect either, since the EPP-driven movement is implicated in successive cyclic Ā-movement, as in (4).

(4) When did Paul say [$_{CP}$ ~~when~~ that Pam called her mother ~~when~~]?

In (4), for example, where the initial movement of *when* is driven by an EPP feature on *that*, movement of *when* into a higher position creates an A-bar chain, the head of which is the leftmost, visible token of *when* and the tail of which is the rightmost copy of *when* in the lower clause. To form this chain for interpretation at the LF interface, the intermediate copy in [Spec, C] must be erased. In that case, there will be no specifier for *that* at LF, and so the EPP rule cannot apply at that point in the derivation.

If the EPP is not an interface constraint, then it must be a rule that constrains the form of derivations. This is the reason Chomsky (2000) reinvents the EPP as a feature to be checked on T (and other heads). But Chomsky's implementation of the EPP as an uninterpretable feature is not proof against the same sort of problems as beset the purely representational statements of the EPP, although the issues are subtle. (It should be said that Chomsky's discussion of the problem is rather more programmatic than detailed, so the target I am confronting here may be as much a strawperson as it is a representation of Chomsky's views. Nevertheless, the issues can only become clearer by working through them.)

For Chomsky, movement does not involve making a new copy of the moved phrase; instead, the same phrase comes to occupy two (or more) positions in the phrase marker.[3]

Notice that even in this model, the EPP feature remains representational, in the sense that it is to be deleted only when the phrase marker provides something to occupy the specifier position for the probe in question. In other words, the right structure must first be formed, and then it is examined to ensure that the probe head has a specifier. If the phrase marker (representation) fails this test, the EPP feature remains intact, crashing the derivation. As Roberts and Roussou (1998) observe, positing this type of feature to characterize movement is inherently non-explanatory, since the feature does little more than point to the effect of movement.

Because the EPP "feature" remains a representational rule at heart, its effects could even be replicated by a phrase structure rule. Rather than requiring that TP have a specifier, we could derive the same results by stipulating that the final form of TP must adhere to the following pattern: TP → DP T'. This rule would simply have to take effect before TP could be allowed to merge with something else to build up the phrase marker further.

On the one hand, the obviously stipulative nature of the EPP is convenient, inasmuch as the concept serves as a placeholder within the theory for something that everyone can agree is missing an explanation, making it easier to address other theoretical questions without being sidetracked. But on the other hand, we would like to actually find an explanation, or at least make progress toward one.

Besides the broad conceptual problems raised by the EPP, there is a substantial empirical problem concerning the status of head movement in the derivation. If syntactic movement involves only the creation of new specifiers, then head movement either does not exist, or it is not actually syntactic. Chomsky (2000) claims the latter, and concludes that head movement can be excluded from the (narrow) syntactic derivation. The phenomena that syntactic head movement operations might explain must then be explained by parallel operations in the mapping from syntax to the PF interface—that is, by "stylistic" or morphological rules.

But the existing literature provides abundant evidence that head movement truly is syntactic, at least some of the time. Most compelling to my mind is the type of phenomenon discussed by Baker (1988), in which noun, verb, and preposition incorporation interact with Case assignment. As Baker shows, incorporation can extend the domain over which Case assignment may take place. But if Case assignment is a side effect of valuation of ϕ-features, which itself must involve a probe-goal relation, then Case must be assigned within the (narrow) syntactic derivation. And if incorporation has an effect on this aspect of the derivation, then incorporation cannot be delayed until the postsyntactic PF mapping. So at least the incorporation type of head movement must be syntactic. (Zwart (2001) develops an argument to the same effect involving verb-second inversion head movement in Germanic.)

If head movement must form part of the derivation, then the conception of movement as always driven by EPP features is simply incomplete.

In this work, I present a partially new model of the basic movement operation in syntax—partially new because it is mostly a reassembling of ideas that have been suggested elsewhere in the literature, but that have not, I believe, been put together in the precise manner that I present here. The unifying concept in this model is the operation of *provocation*, which occurs in the course of feature valuation when certain *probes* seek a value for their unvalued features by identifying a goal to supply what they lack. Provocation forces the generation of a copy of the goal; the copy originates outside the original phrase marker, and it must then be reintroduced into it in various ways. In this approach, movement is not forced by the need for extra positions—extra positions are generated because movement is taking place.

Unlike an EPP feature, or its historical antecedents, provocation drives movement to a specifier position or to a head position with the same mechanism. In fact, it is built into the notion of provocation that the two cannot be separated. If one is possible, so is the other.

The following chapters develop this idea in various ways. Chapter 2 presents the central proposal, and shows how it can be implemented in the analysis of a variety of familiar cases of syntactic movement. The emphasis here is on broad coverage rather than detailed exposition of particular constructions. In chapters 3 and 4, a series of case studies is presented. Chapter 3 demonstrates the effects of provocation in various inversion constructions: quotative, negative, interrogative, and Germanic verb-second. Chapter 4 presents a detailed analysis of Germanic embedded clause structure, in which provocation within the "left periphery" is shown to explain the distribution and intricacies of various types of complementizers across the language family. In chapter 5, the focus is on the details of chain formation and successive cyclic movement in a provocation model.

Throughout, I assume a basic familiarity with current work in minimalist syntactic theory and with the accompanying terminology.

How this all works can be illustrated readily with some of the more familiar cases of movement. Take movement of the subject from inside a verb phrase to the [Spec, T] position, as in (1).

(1) [TP Jenny was [vP *t* putting up the tent]]

At an earlier point in the derivation of this sentence, the structure was (2).

(2)

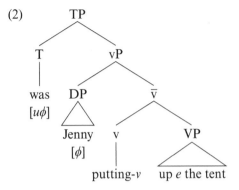

The T head of TP bears unvalued ϕ-features in (2), and these must be valued (and deleted) in order for the derivation to converge. The ϕ-features in T therefore act as a probe that seeks a matching set of features in the vP complement to T. Because *Jenny* is part of the vP and bears ϕ-features, the probe identifies the features of *Jenny* as a *match*, hence, as a potential goal. But there is more to be said about the ϕ-features in T in the derivation of (1). Not only are the ϕ-features unvalued; they are also provocative. And a provocative feature, or feature set, is not satisfied by finding a value—it also affects the phrase that it matches by requiring that a copy be made of that phrase.[3] Thus the result of the feature matching, valuation, and provocation by T is the new pair of structures in (3).

(3)

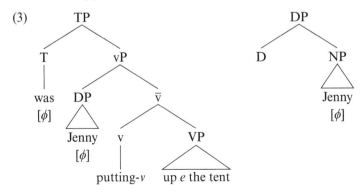

Despite the two distinct "positions" occupied by the two copies of the *Jenny* DP, the pair still counts as a single syntactic unit, a chain, with respect to θ-role assignment and other issues of semantic interpretation. Following Frampton and Gutmann 2000, I suppose that the φ-features of *Jenny* are shared by the two copies, and I hypothesize that this suffices to establish shared chain membership, at least for the purposes of θ-role assignment. (This supposition is supported more rigorously below.) Any operation that affects the features of one, such as Case assignment, will therefore necessarily affect the features of the other at the same time. (The semantic impact of feature-sharing operations is later minimized by deletion of shared features from positions in which they are not interpretable (Pesetsky and Torrego 2007).)

Since two separate phrase markers cannot be interpreted, a merge operation must next, and immediately, unify the two components of (3) into the single phrase marker (4).

(4)

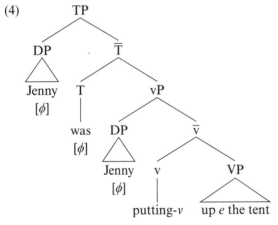

And within this familiar structure, the usual conventions of PF and LF interpretation may apply. Thus the lower copy of *Jenny* will be stripped of phonetic content, and only the upper one pronounced.

It should be immediately apparent what the significant differences are between the model of movement developed here, and any model based on some form of the EPP. In the provocation model, no reference is made to any need to "fill" a specifier position, or to occupy a phrasal edge. Instead "movement" is a side effect of the creation of a second copy of a single phrase. The fact that movement will often make use of a specifier position is simply the automatic consequence of how two separate phrase markers are unified by external merge. If there is another way to unify two separate phrase markers—such as adjunction of one to the other—then we might expect movement to sometimes make use of this second structure-building operation as well. If this occurs—and I will argue at length that it does—then it does so without any alteration in the original triggering mechanism, which will still simply ensure that a pair of phrase markers must be unified.

2.2 The Inner Workings of Provocation

The *effect* of provocation is a binary structure like (5), in which (β', β) constitute a chain, and from which a resulting structure will be formed in which β' merges at the root or head of HP.

(5)

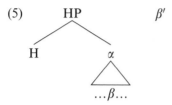

The provocation *mechanism* is simply a fortuitous combination of simplex operations, each of which has been proposed elsewhere in the literature. The feature valuation operation lies at the heart of provocation. Feature valuation occurs only when a probe identifies a matching goal. And the match for a probe can be found either internally, in the complement domain of the probe, or externally, in a separate phrase marker drawn independently from the numeration.

The clearest case of a match situated external to the probe's own phrase marker can be found in some languages with the interrogative pronoun *why*. Rizzi (1996) observes that in Italian questions of this type, the finite verb need not be adjacent to the *wh*-phrase, in contrast to questions with other *wh*-phrases:

(6) a. Perché Gianni è partito?
        why   Gianni is left
    b. *Come Gianni ha parlato?
        how   Gianni has spoken
    c. *Dove Gianni è andato?
        where Gianni is gone

Rizzi (1999) shows that this type of pattern emerges in languages in which the *why wh*-phrase does not undergo *wh*-movement from inside the clause, but instead arrives in the left periphery by external merge. But this then raises the further question of how the unvalued probe feature that normally triggers *wh*-movement can be valued in sentences like (6a).[4] If interrogative C must value its uninterpretable *wh*-feature, it must be able to find a matching goal. But the only *wh*-phrase available in (6a) never occupies a position in the domain of C at any point in the derivation. It follows that the C probe must be able to match features in a phrase *external* to the phrase marker, which is then merged at the root to CP.[5]

(7)

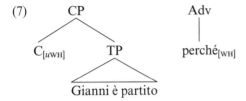

In many languages, expletive subjects must also be able to serve as goals external to the phrase marker of the probe. A fairly clear example of this involves impersonal passives in French.

(8) (Kayne and Pollock 2001)
   Il a été procédé au réexamen de la loi.
   it has been proceeded to-the reexamination of the law

In (8), the ϕ-features of T appear to be valued by *il*, and presumably T Case-marks *il* in the process. There is no other nominal available in this structure that T might take as the goal, *réexamen* being the Case-marked complement of the preposition *à*. The alternative would be that the finite verb in a structure like this simply bears default third-person singular agreement, because it does not agree with anything at all, but this alternative requires that some extra account be given of the obligatory presence of the expletive in this sentence. What is more, if T does not agree with expletive *il* when it is present, then it is difficult to account for the fact that T *cannot* agree with plural postverbal subjects in unaccusative sentences like (9).

(9) Il a/*ont été élu plusieurs candidats du Parti Vert.
   it has been elected several candidates of-the Party Green

On the other hand, if the ϕ-features of T find a match in *il* external to the original TP phrase marker, then both the obligatory presence of the expletive and the absence of agreement by T with anything else follow immediately.

   (Selectional features might also be analyzed as probes that require an external match. Chomsky (2000) speculates that selection is equivalent to attraction, inasmuch as both involve a head trying to situate another phrase at its edge. The implementation of this idea in terms of provocation would be slightly different, since the feature valuation is distinct from the subsequent merge operation in this model. If selectional features are probes, then they would be valued by the generation of an external phrase with the appropriate categorial properties. Merge of the goal in this valuation procedure would be necessary in order to create a unique phrase marker before the derivation continues. The consequence would be the presence of a phrase at the edge of its selecting head, but this would be the result of provocation, not its cause. The empirical effects would be the same as in other theories of selection, it seems.)

From a certain perspective, a match between a probe and an external goal makes more sense as a component of grammar than does matching with internal goals. Consider the effect of external valuation of a $[u\text{WH}]$ feature on C in a *why* question. If interrogative C lacked such a feature in a language like English or Italian, then there would be no salient signifier at the clause edge to mark that clause as a question. With the $[u\text{WH}]$ probe present, however, some goal must be found that can convey this information. So the presence of an unvalued feature in C provides a means to ensure that a question can be readily identified as such. Internal valuation has no such effect, since the goal does not occupy the (left) edge, and does not replace the probe at that edge.

External matching operations make better sense in terms of computational efficiency as well. When internal matching occurs, the probe must conduct a search within its complement for the goal, and the preferred goal is the one found by the minimal search. But with external matching, the goal is already identified. No search is necessary.

Chomsky's (2001) proposal that external merge is preferable to movement makes sense in these terms. He observes that expletive *there* must be used to fill a subject position if there is an option of either doing so or of moving an internal nominal argument. This accounts for the contrast in (10).

(10) a. *There seems a ship to have landed.
     b. There seems to have landed a ship.

In Chomsky's analysis, the subject position in the complement clause in (10a) is filled by moving *a ship* even though the presence of *there* in the numeration for the same phase might have been chosen. If *there* is chosen instead, as in (10b), the result is grammatical.

If the T probe must value ϕ-features in raising complements, then this pattern follows directly from efficient search requirements. If *there* is drawn from the numeration to serve as the goal to value T, then no search is necessary.[6] In contrast, in order to displace *a ship*, a search must be conducted to find the closest goal within the complement of T.[7]

Johns (2000) claims that language design exhibits a crosslinguistic balance between morphological expression and expression by displacement. In other words, the same concepts are expressed morphologically in some languages and by movement in others. If this is accurate, then we would want formal theory to provide a reason why this state of affairs should obtain. Again, the idea that unvalued features match external goals suggests what the reason might be. At least some unvalued features might correspond to concepts that are not capable of being fully expressed by the morphology of a certain head in a given language, where other languages might express that concept effectively using their morphological resources. The way to enable expression in languages that lack particular morphological tools then would be by finding an external match for the particular feature to merge locally. In effect, this would provide a means of supplementing weak morphology with extra phrasal structure.

I do not mean to imply that a functional explanation is all that we require to explain why *wh*-phrases might appear at the clause edge. Any explanation of this type must obviously take for granted the presence in the grammar of the formal mechanisms that may be used to functional ends. But functional pressures presumably have some role to play in explaining how the resources supplied by universal grammar are deployed in the development of actual (I-)languages.

Of course, most types of *wh*-phrases cannot be used simply as an external match for unvalued [*u*WH] features. Most *wh*-movement is not just external merge. The use of *who* or *what* in this way is clearly impossible: (11)

(11) *Who/what Joan repaired the drill.

Unlike *why*, which can apparently be interpreted (semantically) by binding some element in the event structure of a lower clause, *who* and *what* must belong to a well-formed operator-variable chain structure in order to fulfill their semantic functions. The unacceptability of (11) reflects the absence of any such chain for *who/what*.

Fortunately, there is a second way for probes to find an external match that allows for the formation of operator-variable chains. It is clear from the phenomenon of Across-the-Board movement that a probe may match more than one goal at a time. Simultaneous matching occurs both with A-movement and with Ā-movement.

(12) a. Jean should [_____ visit the exhibit] and [be entertained _____
       by the guide].
     b. Which article has [Marcel proofed _____] and [Dan reviewed
       _____]?

Simultaneous matching of this type is possible only when neither goal is
closer than the other to the probe. "Closeness" is evidently defined relative to a section of the phrase marker, and not absolutely. In other words,
it does not matter if there are more categories separating the probe and
goal in one conjoined phrase than there are in the other. Relative distance
is not compared further once the bifurcation of conjoined structures takes
place.

Since a single probe can match multiple goals in one operation, it is
possible in principle for a probe to match an external goal and an internal
goal at the same time. Consider the structure (13), where C is interrogative and must find a match for its unvalued [uWH] feature.

(13) [$_{CP}$ C$_{[u$WH$]}$ [$_{TP}$ Beth danced with who$_{[$WH$]}$]]

There are three different ways this might occur. C could simply find its
match internally, because *who* carries the appropriate [WH] feature. The
result of valuation would then be the same structure as in (13), except
that the features of C would now be valued. Alternatively, the C probe
could match an external *wh*-phrase, in which case a structure like
(14) could be generated, following valuation and merge of the external
wh-phrase.

(14) [$_{CP}$ why$_{[$WH$]}$ C$_{[$WH$]}$ [$_{TP}$ Beth danced with who$_{[$WH$]}$]]

The third way for valuation of the probe to occur is with a simultaneous
matching of the [uWH] probe with two goals. C can match an external
who and the internal *who* at the same time, and thereby take on the value
of both of them simultaneously. The resulting structure will then be (15).

(15) [$_{CP}$ who$_{[$WH$]}$ C$_{[$WH$]}$ [$_{TP}$ Beth danced with who$_{[$WH$]}$]]

Notice that this procedure does not yet ensure that the structure will be
interpretable at LF. In fact, there is no particular difference between the
structure (15) and the ungrammatical structure (16) unless something unifies the two instances of *who* in the former.

(16) [$_{CP}$ what$_{[$WH$]}$ C$_{[$WH$]}$ [$_{TP}$ Beth danced with who$_{[$WH$]}$]]

I propose that the valuation operation itself is what unifies the internal
and external goal. More precisely, I maintain that simultaneous valuation

In languages that lack partial *wh*-movement, two matching goal phrases must be identical, as they are in English, for example. But in German, evidently, the constraints on chain formation are less restrictive, and a complete *wh*-phrase can form a chain with a bare *was*. So the structure (29) is permitted, in which *was* and *wen* value the [*u*WH] feature of C together.

(29) [$_{CP}$ C [$_{TP}$ du glaubst [$_{CP}$ wen$_{i[WH]}$ C [$_{TP}$ Irina wen$_i$ liebt]]]]

$$\text{was}_{i[WH]}$$

Subsequent merger of the external *wh*-phrase with CP then produces the sentence (27a). Since the external *was* is not identical to the original internal one, the phonetic content of the latter cannot be deleted, and so both *wh*-phrases are pronounced.

For (27b), of course, a similar derivation will occur. The only important difference is that there are two points in the derivation for *was* to be introduced above *wen*.

In short, the existence of partial *wh*-movement appears quite unproblematic in the approach advocated here, and simply reflects a degree of parametric variation in chain formation.

Other marked options in *wh*-movement appear to be more amenable to analysis in this framework, too. For example, *wh*-movement of clitics presents a challenge to EPP-based analyses, but is easy to accommodate into a provocation account. Since phrasal movement displaces (copies of) relatively large constituents, the normal effect is creation of a specifier at the root. Occasionally, however, phrasal movement produces an adjunction structure instead. This plausibly occurs when *wh*-movement affects French *que*, the clitic allomorph of *quoi* (Bouchard and Hirschbühler 1986).

(30) a. Qu'a   vu   Jean?
         what-has seen Jean
         'What did Jean see?'

    b. (Poletto and Pollock 2004)
         *Que, d'après toi, a   vu   Jean?
         what according to you has seen Jean
         'What, according to you, has John seen?'

    c. (Poletto and Pollock 2004)
         Qui, d'après toi, a   vu   Jean?
         who according to you has seen Jean
         'Who, according to you, has Jean seen?'

(31) a. *Que et   qui a-t-elle vu?
         what and who has she seen
         'What and who has she seen?'
      b. À quoi et   à qui a-t-elle pensé?
         to what and to who has she thought
         'What and who has she thought of?'

As Bouchard and Hirschbühler show, *que* must be adjacent to verbal support to its immediate right, just as are the pronominal clitics in French. Other *wh*-words in the language are not constrained in this way.

It is possible to approach such data from a different angle, and treat it as a purely prosodic effect. In such a vew, the special property of *que* would simply be that it must be left-adjacent to a verb to form a legitimate prosodic bond, regardless of the syntactic position *que* occupies. In that case, though, we would expect the status of conjoined *que* to improve if it appears on the right, as in (32), which is not the case.

(32) *Qui et que a-t-elle vu?

If it is right to take *que* to be a clitic syntactically, then it requires a position other than the specifier position that other *wh*-phrases typically occupy. And in that case, *wh*-movement of *que* cannot be driven by the need to create a specifier, as the usual story has it. In the model I am proposing, a provocative feature of C provokes *que* so that a new copy of *que* is situated alongside the original CP phrase marker:

(33) [$_{CP}$ C$_{[uWH]}$ [$_{TP}$ a vu que$_{[WH]}$ Jean]]

              que$_{[WH]}$

The new copy of *que* must then merge with CP, but its clitic character requires that the result of this merger be an adjunction structure. This particular property of *que* is sufficient to overrule the usual preference for specifier creation, so *que* adjoins to C instead of becoming its specifier.[9]

In this analysis, the attachment of *que* as a clitic is not directly connected to the forces that compel movement. Provocation has the same immediate effect on specifiers and clitics—it ensures that an external copy is generated. For this reason, the *que* can behave as both a specifier and a clitic within one derivation. When long *wh*-movement of *que* occurs, all but the final steps in successive cyclic movement will involve creation of a specifier in CP. In (34), where *que* originates as the object of *faire* in the complement clause, the complementizer *que* will provoke the interrogative pronoun, which then can merge at the CP root as a specifier.

(34) Qu'a   dit Louise que tu   as   fait?
     what has said Louise that you have done
     'What did Louse say that you did?'

In fact, given the overall preference for merging phrases as specifiers, clitic *que must* merge into [Spec, C] in the complement clause, since it will not actually have its PF realization in that position. Later provocation by root C will again produce a simple copy of *que*, but the following merge operation will have a different effect, because *que* is pronounced in the root clause, so it must occupy a clitic position at that point. But the provocation operation itself does exactly the same thing at each point.

The grammars of various South German dialects also include *wh*-elements that appear to raise to a clitic position instead of a specifier. Bayer and Brandner (2008) show that certain small interrogative pronouns in these dialects are incompatible with overt *dass* complementizers in embedded questions, although larger *wh*-phrases can co-occur with *dass*. Bavarian examples of this pattern appear in (35).

(35) a.   I frog-me, fia wos dass-ma an zwoatn Fernseher braucht.
          I ask-REFL for what that-one a second TV   needs
          'I wonder what one needs a second TV for.'
     b.   I hob koa Ahnung, mid was fia-ra Farb dass-a zfrien
          I have no idea   with what for-a color that-he content
          waar.
          would-be
          'I have no idea with what color he would be happy.'
     c.   *I woass aa ned, wer dass allas am Sunndoch in da Kiach
           I know too not who that all   at Sunday   in the church
          gwen is.
          been is
          'I don't know either who all has been to church on Sunday.'

In (35c), the *wh*-word cannot co-occur with *dass*. Bayer and Brandner analyze this pattern as movement of an atomic *wh*-phrase to a TP-external position where it can rebrand itself as C and merge with T as the head of CP. Since the *wh*-word is itself the complementizer, there cannot be a second complementizer in the same clause. In the (35a,b) examples, however, normal *wh*-movement displaces full *wh*-phrases to [Spec, C], and an overt complementizer is then possible.

Bayer and Brandner support this analysis by showing that the small *wh*-words behave like heads rather than phrases with respect to "*n*-intrusion," an Allemanic morphological process that inserts an /n/

between a vowel-final head and a clitic pronoun adjoined to its immediate right. This is possible in embedded clauses in Allemanic when a pronoun appears to the right of a small *wh*-word, but not when it follows a larger vowel-final *wh*-phrase.[10]

(36) a. . . . wa   -n -er tuet.
             what   he does
             '. . . what he does'
     b. . . . wo   -n -er ani   isch
             where   he toward is
             '. . . where he has gone to'
     c. *. . . von wo   -n -er herkommt
             from where   he comes
             'where he comes from'

Such data supports the conclusion that small *wh*-words do not raise to a specifier position under *wh*-movement. In a provocation model, this conclusion is unproblematic. Suppose that words like *wa*, *wo*, *wer* are simply proclitic elements in South German dialects. Provocation of the small *wh*-words by C then will produce a structure in which an external clitic interrogative pronoun must find a place to attach within the CP of the probe. They therefore adjoin to C instead of merging as specifiers with CP. The other differences follow from the structure of the head position, which now includes a clitic element on the left. The contrast in (35) shows that overt *dass* is impossible when there is a clitic adjoined to C. And the possibility of *n*-intrusion in (36a,b) reflects the fact that the proclitic *wh*-word is actually a part of the C to which the pronominal clitic is itself attached.

Multiple *wh*-movement is better suited to a provocation analysis, too. As is now well documented, some languages allow a single head to acquire multiple specifiers in the course of a derivation (Ura 2000; Richards 1997; Hiraiwa 2005). The legitimacy of such derivations must reflect, in part, parametric variation in the probe features that trigger movement. In models in which movement is driven by the EPP, the probe must then require multiple specifiers. In the P-feature model, the nature of this parametric variation will be quite different.

Consider the case of multiple *wh*-movement in Bulgarian, as described by Rudin (1988) and Richards (1997). Movement of a single *wh*-phrase, as in (37a), will take place when the provocative C probe induces simultaneous matching with the internal *wh*-phrase and with an external copy, which then merges at the root to become a specifier in CP.

(37) *Bulgarian* (Richards 1998)
    a. Koj e   vidjal Pjotr.
       who [AUX] seen Peter
       'Who saw Peter?'
    b. Koj kogo e   vidjal.
       who whom [AUX] seen
       'Who saw whom?'

In (37b), the same type of probe induces movement of both *wh*-phrases. This means that the ability of the probe to produce a binary chain in Bulgarian is not exhausted by a single provocation event. I will use the term *agitator* to characterize provocative probes of this type. As a matter of parametric choice, then, Bulgarian C is an agitator, with a provocative [WH] feature.

Agitation is subject to the same reliance on a prior matching operation as is a single provocation event. So only *wh*-phrases may be provoked by the second (and subsequent) provocations in a Bulgarian multiple-*wh* question.

The technical details of agitation are far from clear, but we may hypothesize a scenario like the following. An agitator must originate as a provocative probe with normal unvalued features. For example, Bulgarian C in both of the (37) examples must enter the derivation with a provocative [uWH] feature. The probe matches its unvalued feature with both an external and an internal goal, which then value the probe and form a chain structure in the process. In (37a), the [WH] feature of C is then dispensable, and it can be deleted. However, in (37b) the same probe feature has more work to do with respect to the remaining *wh*-phrase in its domain. It must therefore be allowed to lose the value that it acquired in the earlier valuation process, so that it may provoke the next *wh*-phrase *kogo* in its domain.

An agitator is then a provocative feature that is permitted to *forget* a value that has been assigned by an earlier valuation operation. Notice, though, that the feature valuation that renders C interpretable for PF always takes place with the first such match, and is not affected by subsequent matching operations. Therefore, it must be the case that "Spell-Out" of the features of the probe takes place immediately after valuation, so that these features may be reused in subsequent provocations of the same type.

Agitation involves the reuse of a single probe in multiple valuations; the effect of multiple provocations on the structure of the phrases involved is a separate issue. What is necessary for a derivation involving agitation to succeed is simply that some way must be found to incorporate each of the new external goal phrases into the original phrase marker. This may involve creation of multiple specifiers, but there are other possible outputs as well. As Richards (1997) observes, the second (and any subsequent) *wh*-phrase in the Bulgarian multiple-*wh* questions is "tucked in" to a specifier position to the right of the first. This reflects a structure-building principle that is evidently independent of the provocation operations.

Agitation may also produce structures in which the goals are displaced to nonspecifier positions. One example of an agitator that does not generate multiple specifiers may be the T that hosts nonsubject clitics in the Romance languages. Consider the French examples in (38).

(38) a. Marc a   emprunté ces   skis de   Joanne.
        Marc has borrowed these skis from Joanne
     b. Il   a   emprunté ces   skis de   Joanne.
        she has borrowed these skis from Joanne
     c. Marc les   a   empruntés de   Joanne.
        Marc them has borrowed from Joanne
        'Marc borrowed them from Joanne.'
     d. Il les   en   a   empruntés
        he them of-her has borrowed
        'He borrowed them from her.'

French T is provocative, so the subject nominal that values the ϕ-features of T is provoked, and remerges as [Spec, T] in (38a).

(39)

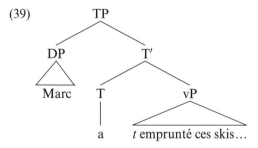

When vP contains pronouns (other than the subject), they also adjoin to T, as in (38c,d).[11] T is moreover an agitator, so after it provokes the subject (and obtains a valuation of its own ϕ-features), it may provoke another, more distant phrase that it matches. Pronouns bear ϕ-features, so they may be provoked by a T agitator. Nonpronominal nominals are

(54) $[_{CP}$ wh x C $[_{TP}$ Shelby was reading x: book(x)]]

My intention, in giving a name to the Refine operation, is to make explicit an idea that is already implied in other approaches to agreement or feature valuation: the idea that something in the LF content of a probe is altered after an agreement operation takes place. Actually, it is made equally explicit by Pesetsky and Torrego (2007), who simply do not identify it by name. In Chomsky's approach, the newly valued probe features are normally stripped away entirely by the Transfer operation, which applies once valuation has taken place; Refine is therefore a component of a more complex Transfer operation.[17] In some form or other, the Refine operation seems inescapable. The only thing that I am adding to this is the idea that it is not only the probe that is affected by deleting uninterpretable content. Everything in a chain is subject to the same process.

In a language like German, where partial *wh*-movement may occur, the lexicon seems to provide a *wh*-phrase that need not be affected by the Refine operation. Consider again example (27a).

(27) a. Was glaubst du wen Irina liebt?
        what believe you who Irina loves
        'Who do you believe that Irina loves?'

The use of *was* in this sentence does not imply nonanimacy in the answer to the question being asked. The meaning of *was* in this type of question is somehow less rich than it would normally be. This follows if partial *wh*-movement involves the use of *wh*-words that come from the lexicon in a "pre-Refined" form. In other words, the meaning of *was* when it is introduced into the derivation is already that of a pure operator—[wh x]—that carries no extra information about the restrictions on the range of the variable. When valuation forms a chain with this type of element, the Refine operation is able to leave it in the same state it was in beforehand.

With pure A-movement, the formation of an *n*ary chain is slightly different. Consider the movement of the subject in a simple intransitive sentence:

(55) a. $T_{[u\phi]}$ $[_{vP}$ Jennifer$_{[\phi]}$ laughed]
     b. $T_{[\phi]}$ $[_{vP}$ $[_{DP}$ Jennifer$_{i[\phi]}$] laughed]

        <u>$[_{DP}$ Jennifer$_{i[\phi]}$]</u>
     c. $[_{TP}$ Jennifer$_{i[\phi]}$ T $[_{vP}$ ~~Jennifer$_{i[\phi]}$~~ laughed]]

Formation of A-chains leaves full semantic content in the head and tail positions. This is why "quantifier lowering" effects arise in A-chains but not in Ā-chains (May 1977).

We may attribute the different semantic effects of the Refine operation to differences in the probes that trigger the complex provocation operation. When an A head contains the P-feature, the result is a pure copying operation, in which a chain is formed with identical (semantic) content in the head and foot. When an Ā head like C provokes, the result is a chain with complementary, quantificational content in the head and foot.

2.6   Provoking Head Movement

It should already be clear that the provocation model provides an account of movement to specifier positions that has coverage at least equivalent to the standard EPP model for standard cases of A and Ā movement. What will be of interest in what follows is how the P-feature model differs from the standard model in the analysis of head movement. In the simplest cases, as we have seen, P-features will always trigger movement to specifier or clitic positions. But sometimes, P-features can trigger head movement instead. And sometimes, the derivation can induce a flip from a specifier movement context to a head-movement context.

A number of conditions must be satisfied before this situation will arise. First, because the computational component prefers phrasal movement to head movement, a goal feature must be located somewhere where full phrasal movement is not possible.[18] As already discussed, this appears to involve cases where the goal is found in the head of the complement to a P-head.

(56)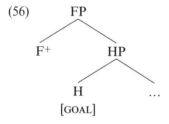

Second, there must be no equidistant phrase that also contains features matching the probe.

An important feature of this model is that the size of the phrase to be copied may vary depending on the syntactic context, even though the same basic provocation operation is responsible for making sure there is an external match of *some* size. When a provocative probe matches features in the head of its complement, the size of the copy shrinks dramati-

made of some category that contains *v*, which would then need to merge in [Spec, T] for the derivation to proceed successfully.

(60)

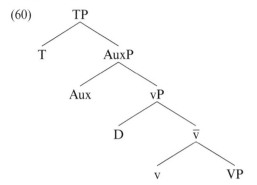

The central cases of the Head Movement Constraint (Travis 1984) thus follow automatically in this model.

Incorporation phenomena will follow the same pattern. Baker's (1988) demonstration that noun incorporation is syntactic is compelling, but it leaves unanswered some important questions about how incorporation is driven within the derivation. Working in a Government-and-Binding framework, Baker was able to assume that movement may occur whenever the result is a suitable representation. In that model, it was sufficient to suppose that the verbs that incorporate are morphologically suitable hosts for incorporation, so that the process might take place freely when necessary. And then principles like the Case filter do the rest.

If movement must be driven by some force, as I assume, then this must be as true for incorporation as it is for A-movement or *wh*-movement. So Baker's model requires an update.

Consider the well-studied noun incorporation structures of Southern Tiwa (Allen, Gardiner, and Frantz 1984). In this language, nouns originating in the domain of the verb can be incorporated. All such inanimate nouns must be incorporated, as in (61a), and nonproper animate nouns may be (61b,c), and they must be when they are otherwise not Case-marked, as in (61d,e) (Baker 1988).

(61) *Southern Tiwa* (Allen, Gardiner, and Frantz 1984)
    a. Te-shut-pe-ban.
       1s:C-shirt-make-PAST
       'I made the shirts.'
    b. Yedi seuanin bi-mũ-ban.
       those man:PL 1s:B-see-PAST
       'I saw those men.'

    c. Yedi bi-seuan-mũ-ban.
        those 1s:B-man-see-PAST
        'I saw those men.'
    d. Ka-'u'u-wia-ban.
        1s:2s|A-baby-give-PAST
        'I gave you the baby.'
    e. I-'u'u-kur-'am-ban.
        1s:2s-baby-hold-cause-PAST
        'I made you hold the baby.'

It is clear that the verb itself does not require incorporation to be well formed, as the nonincorporating (61b) shows. And it would be entirely ad hoc to invent two forms for every verbal root: one affixal, requiring incorporation, and the other nonaffixal.

Let us narrow in on the optional incorporation in (61c). At the VP level, this sentence and its nonincorporating alternate should presumably share the same structure, something like (62).

(62)

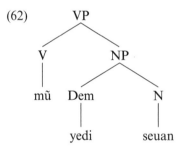

The derivation should evidently be able to produce two outputs from this structure, which suggests that Southern Tiwa has access to an optional rule. Suppose that incorporation takes place when a provocative [uROOT] feature is added to V in the course of the derivation. The [uROOT] feature is valued by a lexical goal, such as the nominal root *seuan*. And since [uROOT] is provocative, there must be an external copy of the nominal root that serves as an extra goal when feature Match takes place. And since the internal goal is the head of the complement to V, it is only the head that is accessible under provocation.

(63)

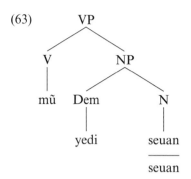

Adjunction of *seuan* to *mũ* then gives rise to the complete incorporation structure of (61c). But since the addition of the provocative [*u*ROOT] feature to V is optional, the unincorporated form in (61b) may be generated, too.

The "optional" addition of [*u*ROOT] becomes effectively obligatory when other factors intervene. Southern Tiwa verbs are able to check Case on only one nominal argument, as Baker (1988) shows. In the double object VP in (61d), and in the causative structure (61e), the verb will Case-mark only the upper of two arguments. The lower argument must therefore be incorporated, by supplying the [*u*ROOT]$^+$ feature to the appropriate verbal root. But the process itself is the same in all cases.

Since head movement and phrasal movement are both reflexes of the same underlying operations, it is not surprising that we find other parallels between these two "types" of movement. For example, head movement sometimes appears to involve "partial" movement, in which the phrase-internal copy is pronounced fully and an external copy that matches it only in part is produced, and then merged. This occurs fairly frequently in noun incorporation languages, where what is incorporated can be something less than a full noun.

Noun incorporation in Plains Cree exhibits this pattern. Full nouns can be incorporated, as "medials," most often when they refer to affected body parts (Wolfart 1971, 1973).

(64) wanih-astimw-ê-w, sak-inisk-ê-n,
     lose-horse-PROC-3T, take/connect-arm-PROC-3,
     nôcih-iskwêw-ê-w
     chase-woman-PROC-3T
     'he loses his horse, he seizes him by the arm, he chases women'

The same medial position in the verb can host "classificatory" morphemes, which must characterize the grammatical object by matching it in semantic features that delimit its physical composition. Thus in (65), the incorporated medial morphemes -*âskw* and -*âpisk* signify that the object is composed of wood and metal respectively.

(65) pakam-âskw-êw,   paw-âpisk-ahwê-w
     strike-wood/CLASS–PROC-3, brush-metal/CLASS-by.tool-3
     'he strikes wood, he brushes it (a metal thing)'

When the context encourages it, both incorporated nouns and incorporated classifiers can be accompanied by lexical objects that contain either another copy of the incorporated noun, or a noun that matches its semantic features.

(66) (Wolfart 2008)
     awa okimâw o-tânisah   ntawih-nôt-iskwêw-âtamiht
     this chief   3-daughter AUX-pursue-woman-PROC
     'Go court this chief's daughter.'

Such copy incorporation represents a head-movement counterpart to *wh*-movement of a partial copy. Consider the structure of the verb phrase prior to incorporation in (66), for the form *pakam-âskw-êw* with the provocative verb stem *pakam* introduced to the structure.

(67) [$_{VP}$ nôt$_{[uROOT]}$ [$_{DP}$ okimâw otânisah$_{[ROOT]}$]]

The probe must match an external goal with a valued [ROOT] feature, but this external goal will be interpretable only by forming a chain with the object nominal in (67). It must therefore match the object in the valuing root feature, and it must be semantically compatible with the object in its own semantic features. Evidently, the match is close enough in Cree as long as the external goal has the right features of physical composition or personal identity. Therefore the external goal *iskwêw* can value the probe together with the direct object, to form the paired structure (68).

(68) [$_{VP}$ nôt$_{[ROOT]}$ [$_{DP}$ okimâw otânisah$_{i[ROOT]}$]]

     iskwêw$_{i[ROOT]}$

Subsequent adjunction of the external goal then produces the attested morphological structure.

   Multiple incorporation structures are also possible, apparently. Collins (2002) shows that †Hoan "compound verbs" are actually underlying serial verb structures in which *v* attracts *both* lexical verbs from their original position inside the verb phrase. Example (69) is derived from the underlying structure (70) by movement of V_1 and V_2 to *v*.

(69) Ma a-   q‖hu ǀ’o   djo   ki   kx’u na.
     1SG PROG pour put.in water PART pot in
     'I am pouring water into the pot.'

(70)

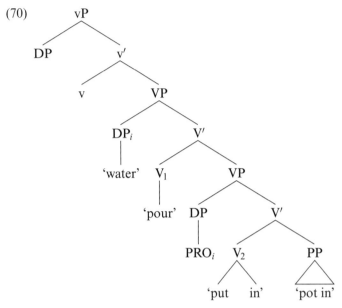

Again, this process falls quickly into place in the current model. In this case, the provocative feature resides in *v*, which is moreover an agitator. So provocation of the closest verb values the [ROOT] feature of *v*, but this probe can then reuse the same feature to match a second external goal. The effect is the formation of two distinct V-chains, each of which originally contains an external verb and an internal one. The external verbs must be incorporated, successively, into the original phrase marker by adjoining to the head. And, as Collins observes, the second adjoined head attaches more closely to the attracting *v*, by "tucking in" to the existing [vP V *v*] head structure.[19]

2.7 Conclusion

More than other movement transformations, head movement has seemed problematic in minimalist approaches (Chomsky 1995, 2000, 2001) in terms of its functional motivation.[20] While Ā-movement clearly contributes to the expressive power of the derivation, and A-movement at least alters scopal relations, head movement appears to be semantically vacuous. As such, one would not expect it to occur at all, at least in the "narrow syntax." If the primary purpose of the derivation is to construct structure for interpretation at the "conceptual-intentional" interface (Chomsky 2007), then the vacuous operations like head movement should be excluded in principle. And yet they occur.[21]

The movement-as-provocation model resolves this apparent dilemma. Head movement does play a part in the narrow syntax, because head movement exists as an inescapable corollary to the existence of phrasal movement. Phrasal movement occurs because probe triggers creation of a copy of its goal, but if the goal is too close, then head movement is the result instead. Phrasal movement cannot be a part of the derivation without head movement becoming possible as well.

3 Provocative Case Studies

The movement model presented in chapter 2 treats movement to specifier positions, clitic positions, and head positions as reflexes of the same fundamental operations. In some configurations, therefore, the situation may arise where provocation may, in principle, trigger head movement, specifier movement, or clitic movement. When this situation occurs, the choice of what movement takes place depends on the details of the local context. One of the factors allowing a choice to be made is a general preference for specifier movement over head movement. But if other factors block specifier movement, then head movement can become the winning option.

This chapter contains a number of case studies in which this situation arises: constructions in which the normal preference for phrasal movement is subordinated by the needs of the derivation, so that head movement takes place instead. To the extent that the derivations for these cases become more transparent in the P-feature model, these constitute evidence that this model is on the right track.

3.1 Quotative Inversion

The major properties of the English quotative inversion construction have been documented by Branigan and Collins (1993), Collins and Branigan (1997), and Collins (1996). In quotative inversion, the usual order of subject and principal verb is reversed, typically when a "quote" appears at the start of the sentence.

(1) a. "Who's on first?" asked Abbott.
   b. "Don't let the cat out!" hollered Gabrielle.
   c. "I love to dance," explained Sam to us.

With Collins and Branigan (1997), I suppose that quotative inversion is triggered when a null quotative operator is preposed. When this occurs, the subject remains in situ and the verb raises past it to a higher head position, presumably T.

(2) "I love to dance." [OP$_i$ [$_T$ explain-ed] [$_{vP}$ Sam t t_i to us]]

The analysis presented in Collins and Branigan 1997 left a number of questions unanswered. The fact that the verb raises to T in this construction is inconsistent with the usual English pattern, and this property of the construction was simply stipulated on the basis of descriptive adequacy. The fact that the subject remains in situ was also left unexplained—it was simply suggested that the presence of the quotative operator somehow removes the EPP feature of T.

Collins (1996) refines that analysis in significant ways. He proposes that the quotative operator is situated in [Spec, T] in (2). Because the presence of the quotative operator is enough to satisfy the EPP feature of T, the subject does not need to raise from its original position. But Collins is unable to shed much light on the fact that the verb raises. He offers only the stipulation (3) (Collins 1996, 41):

(3) The EPP feature of T may enter into a checking relation with the quotative operator only if V[Quote] adjoins to T.

This stipulation nevertheless advances our understanding, inasmuch as it provides an account of the fact that auxiliary verbs are barred from the quotative inversion construction.

(4) *"I love to dance," had explained Sam.

Given (3), the unacceptability of (4) reflects the failure of V[Quote] to license the use of the quotative operator to satisfy the EPP feature of T.

Collins has provided a plausible account of the enforced absence of auxiliary verbs in this construction, I think. But the fact that head movement of the principal verb can occur at all in this construction still remains problematic. Movement requires a motivation and a mechanism. The observation that a quotative verb raised to T may license an operator is in itself not sufficient justification for the movement. The licensing effect is a side effect, not a formal motivation.

Now consider an implementation of these same ideas in a model in which the EPP is reinterpreted in terms of provocation. Let us say that the unvalued ϕ-feature complex of T is provocative, as an inherent property of T. What is more, let us suppose that the principal verb agrees with the agentive subject, presumably as a consequence of internal merge of the subject as a specifier for v. Prior to any movement, the structure of (1c) will be (5).

(5) ("I love to dance") [$_{TP}$ T$^+$ [$_{vP}$ Sam explained OP to us]]

Two problems must be resolved inside TP in order for the derivation to converge. The ϕ-features of T must be valued. And the quotative operator must be raised to the edge of its clause and licensed there by a local quotative verb, in other words by *explain*.

The operator cannot move unless there is an appropriate Match operation. Recall Chomsky's (2000) proposal that movement will often be driven by the addition—in the course of a derivation—of appropriate features to a head, where these (P-)features both check features on a goal in their domain and attract that goal up to specifier position. Let us suppose that this type of operation drives movement of the quotative operator in (5). This will not be a case of adding a P-feature to the head of a phase, since TP is not phasal. Instead, the P-feature is added to T when the derivation can be improved by doing so, by displacing a quotative operator to the edge of TP, where it is presumably in a better position for interpretation. To be specific, let us suppose that a *quotative* P-feature [QT] is added to T, and [QT] attracts the operator up to [Spec, T]:

(6) [$_{TP}$ OP$_i$ T [$_{vP}$ Sam explained t_i to us]]

The option of adding [QT] to T appears to be a marked, language-specific parametric choice. In the sparse literature on comparable constructions in other languages, Swedish (Holmberg 1986) and Spanish (Suñer 2000) both require that the direct quotation, or its null operator, appear external to TP in the left periphery. In these languages, then, it is not permitted to add [QT] to T in the course of the derivation.

The ϕ-features of T must still be valued in (6) to allow convergence, which requires a goal with valued ϕ-features. Both *Sam* and the principal verb *explain* bear valued ϕ-features at this point in the derivation—*Sam* inherently, and *explain* under agreement with *Sam*—so T may select either of these as its goal in Match. If it selects *Sam*, then an external copy of *Sam* must be generated because ϕ-features are provocative, and the copy must then be merged at the root. But T already has a specifier, so there is no convergent continuation of the derivation at this point. If T selects *explain* as its goal, however, the derivation may succeed; a copy is therefore made of *explain* and adjoined to T automatically.

(7) [$_{TP}$ OP$_i$ [$_T$ explain-T] [$_{vP}$ Sam e_v t_i to us]]

Compare the derivation just discussed with that of a clause in which quotative inversion is not involved, such as (8).

(8) Sam explained his passion to us.

At the point where T merges with vP, the structure will be (9):

(9) [$_{TP}$ T [$_{vP}$ Sam explain his passion to us]]

Since no quotative operator needs to be attracted in this case, the only property of T that requires treatment is the unvalued ϕ-feature complex. Again, T may select either *Sam* or *explain* as its goal in Match. This time, however selection of *Sam* is forced because specifier formation is preferred to head movement. Valuation of ϕ in T therefore creates a copy of *Sam*, which is then merged at the TP root:

(10) [$_{TP}$ Sam T [$_{vP}$ *t* explain his passion to us]]

The order of operations is crucial in quotative inversion. If ϕ-feature valuation were to precede the addition of the [QT] feature, then normal subject raising to [Spec, T] would block attraction of the quotative operator. If we suppose that operations are freely ordered at the TP level, then it follows that convergence considerations will force [QT] to be added before ϕ-feature valuation takes place. On the other hand, there may be reason to suppose that the order of operations is not free. In their analysis of Chukchi ergativity, Bobaljik and Branigan (2006) argue that when extra features are added to a head, the extra features must be checked before the original inherent features. If so, then the [QT] feature added to T in quotative inversion will automatically be checked before the inherent ϕ-feature complex can be valued. Either way, the derivational order that leads to a convergent derivation will be forced by general principles. And derivational complexity is reduced, since there will be no need to backtrack to rescue a derivation in which the wrong choice has been made.

Collins's principle (3) relates the verb movement to the way the quotative operator hijacks the EPP feature of T, but without explaining the forces that drive v-to-T movement. In the model just sketched, v-to-T takes place automatically, with the effect that the principal verb will end up in a position where it may plausibly license the quotative operator in [Spec, T]. In sentences where the auxiliary verb appears in T, though, the quotative operator will simply fail to be licensed. As in Collins's account, the ungrammaticality of (4) is due to a failure of licensing, but this simply reflects the fact that compound tenses provide a nonquotative verb as the only head available for attraction by T.

In short, under a P-feature model of "EPP," the major properties of English quotative inversion begin to make sense, which has not been the case in earlier treatments.

3.2 Negative Inversion

The "negative inversion" construction is clearly different from quotative inversion in that it takes place in root and embedded contexts, and it does not involve the principal verb, but only auxiliary verbs (plus *have* and *be*). Nevertheless, it can be shown that the same principles that lead to reversal of word order in quotative inversion are responsible for the word order in examples like (11).

(11) a. No tastier moose stew have I ever sampled.
     b. Never would I support such an amendment.
     c. Only on rare occasions do we stay out late.

Because the inversion involves only auxiliary verbs, it is clear that head movement to a TP external position is implicated in these sentences. And since negative inversion is possible in embedded contexts, as in (12), we must assume that some category smaller than CP is the locus for inversion:

(12) a. I assure you that no tastier moose stew have I ever sampled.
     b. I promise that never would I support such an amendment.
     c. The parents believe that only on rare occasions do we stay out late.

Evidently a complex structure for the "left periphery" is required. Let us take Rizzi's (1997) *articulated CP* model as the structural framework for the analysis.[1] In place of CP, then, I assume that clauses are ForceP (FcP) categories containing FinP complements that in turn contain TP:

(13) [$_{FcP}$ Force [$_{FinP}$ Fin TP]]

Given this much structure, negative inversion can be characterized as a situation in which a negative phrase, or more precisely a monotone-decreasing quantificational expression (Linebarger 1980), is attracted to [Spec, Fin] while T is raised to Fin, as in (14).

(14) [$_{FinP}$ no tastier moose stew$_i$ have-Fin [$_{TP}$ I e ever tasted t_i]]

There is little mystery attached to the movement of the negative phrase in (14). Quantifiers are frequently displaced from their original position, presumably to aid in the formulation of an interpretable LF representation. A-bar movement of *no tastier moose stew* presumably falls into this pattern. And there is no mechanical difficulty in coming up with a characterization of the movement itself. We need only assume some attracting [MD] (monotone-decreasing) feature in Fin, analogous to the [WH] feature that drives *wh*-movement. But movement of T-to-Fin requires an explanation.

Now suppose that Fin, like T, bears provocative unvalued ϕ-features. When Fin merges with TP, the structure of (11a) will be (15).

(15) [$_{FinP}$ Fin$^+$ [$_{TP}$ I have ever tasted no tastier moose stew]]

To raise the negative phrase out of TP, a [MD] P-feature must be added to Fin. So Fin then bears two distinct features (feature complexes) that must be checked: the inherent ϕ-features and the [MD] P-feature. Since the [MD] feature is added to Fin in the course of the derivation, it must be checked first. So [MD] will attract the phrase *no tastier moose stew* to [Spec, Fin], leaving the unvalued ϕ-features still to be checked. The ϕ-features may select either the subject *I* as their goal or the auxiliary verb *have*. (The ϕ-features on *have* will have been valued at an earlier stage in the derivation by agreement with the goal *I*. See Pesetsky and Torrego 2000 for discussion.)[2] But if they select *I*, provocative ϕ will force *I* to be copied and then no merge site is available to host the copy, [Spec, Fin] being already occupied. So *have* must be selected as the goal for valuing the ϕ-features, and a copy of *have* is automatically adjoined to Fin as a result. The T-to-Fin movement simply reflects the way the provocative property of ϕ-features must be satisfied under these particular conditions.

If English permitted multiple specifiers for FinP, then an alternative might be possible, of course. In that case, both the negative phrase and the subject might raise to become specifiers. But English does not permit such structures, possibly as a result of setting some parameter to this effect. This restriction must be set at one of the interface levels, and presumably at PF, where the option of interpreting multiple specifiers in a linear ordering may plausibly be rejected.[3]

The implication of this analysis is that movement to [Spec, Fin] must occur when inversion does not. So in (16), for example, the subject must occupy [Spec, Fin], and not [Spec, T], as is usually assumed.

(16) This is an ordinary sentence.

Since specifiers are preferred to head movement, the subject *this* in (16) must be selected as the goal to value the ϕ-features of Fin, and then the copy of *this* will be merged at the FinP root. Given the arguments of Branigan (1992, 1996b) and Holmberg and Platzack (2005), I suppose that this analysis of simple sentences is unproblematic, and that subjects will generally occupy the [Spec, Fin] position in simple declarative clauses.[4]

One test in English for Ā status confirms this supposition. Progovac (1992) observes that *only*-phrases may license negative polarity items, but only if they occupy an Ā position in "Comp."

(17) a. Only his sister would Jim let borrow a red cent.
   b. *Jim would let only his sister borrow a red cent.
   c. Only four people will Jane invite to any dinner party.
   d. ??Jane invites only four people to any dinner party.

But *only*-phrases that function as subjects appear to be exempt from this constraint:

(18) Only experienced campers are allowed to pitch any tents in this park.

If subjects occupy [Spec, Fin], as I claim, then examples like (18) are not exceptional at all, since the subject actually does occupy an Ā position.

A corollary is that no T-to-Fin movement will be expected when the subject itself is the negative phrase. If [MD] is added to Fin simply in order to attract a negative phrase out of TP, then this operation is redundant for subject negative phrases, which raise to [Spec, Fin] anyway. Thus no *do*-support is possible in a sentence like (19):

(19) *No kinder stranger did ever offer me assistance.

Notice that movement of the negative phrase to [Spec, Fin] is driven by different forces than movement of subjects to the same position in this model. Movement of the former takes place because extra computational "effort" (the extra P-feature) is expended to ensure that the negative phrase is displaced from TP. Presumably this extra effort is justified on semantic grounds, by allowing for a special focus interpretation of the preposed phrase at LF. In contrast, the subject raises to [Spec, Fin], when it does so, simply as a mechanical side effect of the properties of unvalued provocative ϕ-features in Fin. No special interpretation accompanies the movement of the subject to [Spec, Fin], despite its Ā-movement status. And none of the usual tests for Ā-movement (weak crossover, reconstruction effects) are likely to be applicable, simply because the [Spec, T] origin and the [Spec, Fin] landing site are so close to each other.

Rizzi (1996) takes the apparent subject/nonsubject asymmetry in (20) to be an ECP effect, where the subject trace is not properly governed in (20c).

(20) a. I think that never did he help her.
   b. ??The woman who I think that never did he help
   c. *The man who I think that never did help her

An ECP-free account of the same data is possible in the present frame-work. Consider the structure of FinP in the bottom clause in (20c) before Fin provokes anything:

(21)

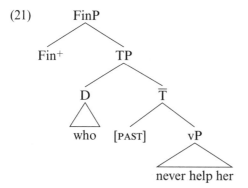

Both *who* and *never* are potential heads of Ā chains in (21), and so each should be raised out of TP if possible. If no extra feature is added to Fin, then the inherent ϕ-features will attract the subject automatically. To at-tract the negative focus *never*, an extra [MD] feature would need to be added to Fin. Because adding the extra feature does not actually improve the structure—since there would still remain one Ā phrase inside TP—we may presume that the derivation avoids this option. Negative inversion is then blocked by the existence of a subject *wh*-phrase. The ECP has noth-ing to do with the results.

A variant of this account of negative inversion comes slightly closer to what Rizzi himself has proposed about negative inversions (Rizzi 2004). As Rizzi (1997) has shown, the left periphery of a clause sometimes appears to contain dedicated positions that host phrasal categories inter-preted as foci or topics. There must therefore be the option of merging heads with particular semantic functions in between the Fin and Force positions. A Foc head of this type attracts foci; Top, topics.

The preposed negative phrase in a negative inversion sentence is always interpreted as a focus, so it should occupy [Spec, Foc]. Foc must then bear a provocative [*u*FOC] feature that matches the focal element inside TP.

If the focus raises directly from its TP-internal origin to [Spec, Foc], then there will be no motivation for T to raise to Fin. Since T does raise, we must suppose more steps in the derivation.

The critical moment is when Fin merges with TP, forming the structure (22).

(22)

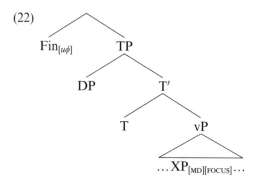

$$\text{Fin}_{[u\phi]} \quad \text{TP}$$
$$\text{DP} \quad \text{T}'$$
$$\text{T} \quad \text{vP}$$
$$\ldots \text{XP}_{[\text{MD}][\text{FOCUS}]} \ldots$$

At this point, it can be determined that two problems will need to be resolved for a successful derivation. The ϕ-features of Fin must be valued, and the focus needs to be displaced into a position appropriate for its focal interpretation. The former can be resolved immediately; the latter cannot, since there is no Foc head available yet. The focus can be displaced, however, if the $[u\text{MD}]^+$ feature is added to Fin. Provocation of the focus will not immediately produce a structure in which the focus occupies the right sort of position, so the derivation may still fail, ultimately, if no Foc head is merged in. But a focus in [Spec, Fin] will always be *closer* to any Foc head that may appear than a focus in [Spec, T] would be. By attracting the focus, Fin therefore eases the demand on the computational machinery at a later point, by ensuring the search for an internal match for Foc will be concluded as quickly as possible. We might think of this procedure as a form of "insurance" that the derivation takes out to keep phrases in a relatively high position when it is known that they will need to move in the end into an Ā position for interpretation anyway. The ϕ-features of Fin can then only be valued with provocation of T, ensuring inverted word order.

Since provocation of the focus by Fin is not actually necessary for the derivation to converge, there are structures in which a focus is displaced without triggering inverted word order. In (23), for example, the focus is attracted directly to [Spec, Foc], without first raising to [Spec, Fin].

(23) Jenny, we invited t already.

The difference reflects a (language-specific) specification that governs what types of provocative features can be added to Fin. In standard English, Fin can take on only the $[u\text{MD}]$ feature. The option of optimizing later search procedures by displacing a focus to [Spec, Fin] is therefore available only when the focus bears a matching $[\text{MD}]$ feature.

Similar remarks will be germane when sentences like (23) are interpreted as topicalization structures, which is possible for some English speakers. Negative inversion is never possible with a topicalization interpretation, however, because monotone-decreasing quantifiers make poor sentence topics.

Root *wh*-questions generally pattern with negative inversion in English, and are in fact susceptible to similar analyses. (Embedded *wh*-questions are quite different, and I defer discussion of their structure to section 4.2.) Like negative phrases, *wh*-phrases are monotone-decreasing quantifiers, so they can be attracted to [Spec, Fin] by the same [MD] feature. Additionally, root *wh*-phrases are plausibly interpreted as sentential foci, so they will be attracted by a Foc head when one is available. So the structures in (24) are generated by the very same mechanisms that have already been expounded here.

(24) a. [FocP when Foc [FinP *t* did-Fin [TP Bev *e* paint this room *t*]]]?
     b. [FocP who Foc [FinP *t* Fin [TP *t* painted this room]]]?

In (24), a provocative [MD] feature is taken on by Fin to attract the *wh*-phrase *when* from within TP, and the provocative ϕ-features of Fin then attract the auxiliary verb. In (24b), the ϕ-features of Fin are enought to attract *who* to [Spec, Fin], so no extra provocative features are required. In both cases, Foc will then attract the *wh*-phrase in [Spec, Fin] to complete the derivation.

French complex inversion patterns with English negative inversion in most respects. Like the English construction, the French involves monotone-decreasing quantifiers, usually negative phrases and *wh*-phrases. And like negative inversion, complex inversion can be derived on two assumptions: first, that French Fin bears provocative ϕ-features inherently, and second, that a provocative [MD] feature can be added to Fin to attract a focus. Thus we find examples like those in (25).

(25) a. Jamais n'aurait-elle   vendu son vélo.
        never   NEG-would-have-she sold   her bike
        'Never would she have sold her bike.'
     b. Quand a-t-il   emprunté son vélo de Suzanne?
        when   has-he borrowed her bike of Suzanne
        'When did he borrow her bike from Suzanne?'

In both cases, the focus is attracted to [Spec, Fin] before raising to [Spec, Foc]. The provocative ϕ-features of Fin can then be satisfied only by provoking T, which consequently raises to Fin.

There are two differences between the English inversion structures and the French. In French, when a subject nominal is left in [Spec, T] instead of raising to [Spec, Fin], it must be pronominal. Lexical DPs in [Spec, T] are unacceptable:

(26) *Jamais n'aurait   Suzanne vendu son vélo.
        Never NEG-would.have Suzanne sold   her bike

I have no explanation for this constraint on lexical subjects in French.

The second difference involves how French grammatically accommodates lexical subjects in complex inversion, by placing them between the *wh*-phrase and the fronted verb, as in (27).

(27) Jamais Suzanne n'aurait-elle   vendu son vélo.
        never   Suzanne NEG-would.have-she sold   her bike
        'Never would Suzanne have sold her bike.'

This word order actually constitutes the most compelling reason to suppose that the quantifier raises from [Spec, Fin] up to [Spec, Foc]. If it did not, there would be no space between it and the verb in Fin in which a subject might be pronounced. But if the quantifier always raises to [Spec, Foc], then the subject may be situated in a Topic Phrase between Foc and FinP. The structure of (27) will then be (28).

(28)

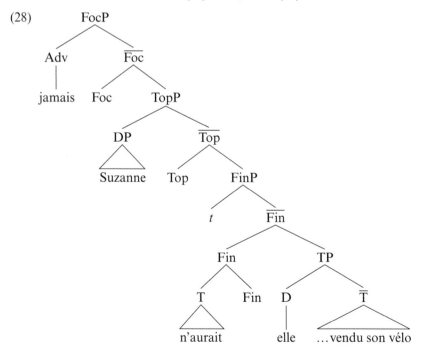

(The subject in [Spec, Top] is presumably interpreted by virtue of a link between it and the pronominal subject in [Spec, T].)

3.3   Germanic Verb-Second Clauses

3.3.1   Topicalization

As is well known, the negative inversion construction is nothing more than a rarified Anglo-French special case of the general Germanic verb-second pattern (Den Besten 1983). Consider the typical Dutch topicalization in (29).

(29)   Dat boek heeft Hans gelezen.
        this book has   Hans read

Sentence (29) displays similar properties to English negative inversion sentences, since the finite verb raises past the subject and the object raises still further to the left. The fronted DP *dat boek* is presumably raising to a TopicP rather than FocP, given the meaning of the sentence (Rizzi 1997). So the structure of (29) may be taken to be (30):

(30)   [$_{TopP}$ dat boek Top [$_{FinP}$ t heeft-Fin [$_{TP}$ Hans t_i gelezen e]]]

The difference in word order between Dutch and English topicalizations can be attributed to the types of P-features that are available to add to Fin. In Dutch, and elsewhere in Germanic, a broader range of phrases can be attracted by Fin, so there must be more P-features than simply the [MD] feature for this purpose. At least one more option must be available: a P-feature that attracts non-monotone-decreasing phrases. Let us refer to this feature as [$\overline{\text{MD}}$].

With this minimal difference between languages in place, the derivation of (29) will proceed as follows. The structure (31) is constructed in the usual way.

(31)   [$_{FinP}$ Fin [$_{TP}$ Hans dat boek gelezen heeft]]

In Dutch as in English, Fin inherently bears provocative unvalued ϕ-features. But the phrase *dat boek* has an active [TOP] feature that will compel its movement out of TP, and Fin must facilitate this movement if it can. So an [$\overline{\text{MD}}$] feature is added to Fin to attract *dat boek* to [Spec, Fin].

Once Fin has attracted its specifier, it must value its ϕ-features. It cannot attract a new specifier, so it chooses the finite verb *heeft* as the goal, and a copy is then made of the finite verb. The copy is then adjoined to Fin. Subsequent merger of Top with FinP will produce the structure in which Top attracts the phrase *dat boek* from [Spec, Fin] up to [Spec, Top], concluding the derivation.

The difference between Dutch and English is minimal as far as the top-icalizing verb-second pattern is concerned. Dutch has access to the [$\overline{\text{MD}}$] feature for attracting phrases to [Spec, Fin], while English permits only the less permissive [MD] feature to be added to Fin. This difference appears to be one that positive evidence would suffice to enable a child to learn, given appropriate guidance from Universal Grammar.[5]

3.3.2 Root *Wh*-Questions

Like negative inversion and Dutch topicalization, root *wh*-questions re-quire inverted word order unless the subject is the *wh*-phrase. And these structures are amenable to the same treatment. A question like (32), for example, is derived with phrasal movement of the *wh*-phrase and head movement of the auxiliary verb.

(32) Where should we meet?

The derivation of (32) therefore involves the following steps. Fin has provocative ϕ-features, and Fin is able to take on an additional provoca-tive feature that attracts *wh*-phrases. (Since *wh*-phrases are monotone-decreasing quantifiers, the [MD] feature that drives negative inversion can play the same role in *wh*-movement.) Fin provokes *where* first, and the new copy of *where* then merges to the [Spec, Fin] position. Fin provokes the auxiliary verb when it values its ϕ-features. The resulting structure is (33).

(33) [$_{\text{FinP}}$ where should-Fin [$_{\text{TP}}$ we *e* meet *t*]]

The other Germanic languages typically form root questions in the same way, as does French (in complex inversion structures). In all cases, Fin provokes a *wh*-phrase first, and then it must satisfy the needs of its original provocative ϕ-features by attracting the finite verb.

Wh-questions differ from negative inversion structures or Dutch topic-alizations in having different shapes in root and embedded clauses. Em-bedded *wh*-questions are typically formed by *wh*-movement that places the *wh*-phrase in [Spec, Force]. (The principles that control the derivation of this type of question are discussed in chapter 4.) But the embedded question structures are not permitted in root contexts. Thus structure (34) is an illegitimate root clause structure.

(34)

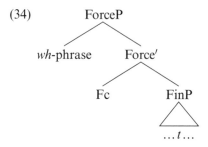

In fact, the necessity of verb-second word order in root questions follows directly from the basic premises of phase theory (Chomsky 2001). Syntactic structure is interpreted cyclically as a phrase is built up. Interpretation takes place automatically on completion of each phase, where phases are at least the ForceP and vP categories. But the entire phase cannot be subject to interpretation, for that would ensure that no movement out of a phase category would ever be possible. Instead, all the structure at the "edge" of a phase, the head and any specifiers, is left alone, while everything contained in the complement of the phase head is interpreted. Thus, given a completed vP phase like (35), everything within VP will be transferred to the PF and LF interfaces, but interpretation of the V-v complex and the agent *Rosanna* will be deferred until the next phase up is completed.

(35)

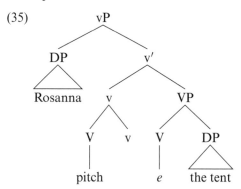

As Fitzpatrick (2006) shows, this algorithm ensures that there must always be uninterpreted phrase structure at the root of a phrase marker; the root must be phasal, and therefore its head and any specifiers cannot be transferred to the interfaces.

For simple declaratives like (36), the consequence is that the Force head can never be interpreted, while everything within FinP will be. (The material within VP will already have been interpreted at an earlier point in the derivation.)

(36)

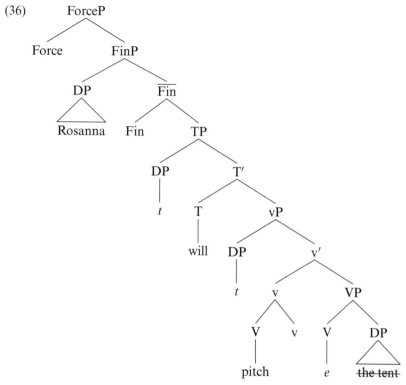

It follows, as well, from the phase interpretation algorithm that a root sentence must always be a phase category—otherwise interpretation of the FinP complement cannot take place at all. So Force is always present in a root clause, even though it can never be given form.

Turning now to the derivation of root questions, we can determine immediately that *wh*-movement cannot be movement to [Spec, Force] in a root clause, because the specifiers for root Force cannot be interpreted, but *wh*-phrases are. Instead *wh*-movement in a root question must raise the *wh*-phrase into a position that remains in the interpreted complement to Force. And in fact there is ample evidence that root *wh*-movement targets a lower position in the left periphery.

Yiddish sometimes permits topicalization in embedded questions. In root questions, this is impossible (Diesing 1990).

(37) *Yiddish* (Moorcroft 1995)
    a. ...vi ikh veys vos bay mir tut zikh
        as I know what by me does itself
       '...as I know what goes on with me'

b. *Ver haynt hot gegesn dos broyt?
   who today has eaten   the bread

c. *Vos hot dem   rov   Max gegebn?
   what has to-the rabbi Max given

With some speakers, the Yiddish pattern can be replicated in English, where monotone-decreasing topics can also (marginally) co-occur with *wh*-phrases in embedded *wh*-structures for clefts.

(38) a.   It was with Mary at the helm that at no time was I concerned about my safety, not with John.

b.   ??The chief would like to know with whom at the helm at no time were you concerned about your safety.

c.   *With whom at the helm at no time were you concerned about your health?

In fact, in English, where topicalization does not require verb-second structure, it can be seen that root *wh*-movement may place the *wh*-phrase in a position to the right of the topic. (This is impossible in embedded questions.[6])

(39) a.   On Tuesday which car did you take?

b.   *I forget on Tuesday which car you took.

Embedded clause *wh*-movement to [Spec, Force] is obviously what it seems to be. Interrogative Force attracts a *wh*-phrase in the usual way; Force must bear a provocative [WH] feature that finds the closest *wh*-phrase as its goal.

Root *wh*-movement must be something different. Since root *wh*-phrases are not in [Spec, Force], and since they appear to the right of topics in [Spec, Top], we must conclude that they occupy either a [Spec, Fin] position or a [Spec, Foc] position in a Focus Phrase situated lower than the Topic Phrase. In other words, root *wh*-movement must be a case of phrasal movement to [Spec, Fin], and perhaps slightly further. The structure of English (40a) and Swedish (40b) are then as shown.

(40) *Swedish*

a.   [$_{FinP}$ Where did [$_{TP}$ I e put the butter t]]?

b.   [$_{FinP}$ Vem pratar [$_{TP}$ Lars e e med t]]?
     who talks   Lars   with

On the whole, the necessity of inversion in root questions is fairly easy to explain, given what has already been said about negative inversion.

The literature includes discussion of one case in which root *wh*-movement in the verb-second languages does not actually produce verb-second word order (Taraldsen 1986b; Åfarli 1986). In some Northern Norwegian dialects, a fronted root *wh*-phrase is followed directly by the subject, as in (41).

(41) *N. Norwegian* (Rice and Svenonius 1998)
Hva du vil drikke til peppersteiken?
what you will drink to the-pepper.steak
'What would you like to drink with the pepper steak?'

Non-verb-second questions of this type are possible for many speakers of these dialects only when the *wh*-word is monosyllabic.

As Rice and Svenonius (1998) show, this phenomenon cannot be fully understood by examining the syntax alone. The prosodic structure is crucial. The general pattern they identify is captured in their constraint (42).[7]

(42) *ProsV2*
The left edge of the verb coincides with the right edge of the first prosodic phrase of the utterance.

Verb-second word order is not permitted in questions when it would ensure a violation of this constraint.

Rice and Svenonius assume that their constraint (42) plays a role in determining whether the verb raises to presubject position. But there is another way to interpret their findings that is consistent with the approach to verb-second word order proposed here. Suppose that this constraint applies only after the narrow syntax has completed its work, because this constraint governs how phrase structure is interpreted at PF. This is a natural role for a prosodic constraint to play, after all. The narrow syntax produces a structure for (41) in which Fin provokes T in the usual way, so that T adjoins to Fin:

(43) [$_{FcP}$ Fc [$_{FinP}$ Hva vil-Fin [$_{TP}$ du e drikke t til peppersteiken?]]]

Adjunction of the verb to Fin in (43) violates the constraint (42), so this sentence will be ungrammatical unless some strategy can be found to repair the structure postsyntactically. One repair strategy that appears to operate in other languages when similar problems arise is reconstruction of a moved phrase to an earlier position, by deleting (some of) the content from the head of a movement chain (Bošković 1997; Bobaljik and Branigan 2006). Since the verbal position is the problem in (43), the most effective repair strategy would be to simply delete the phonetic content of the verb adjoined to Fin, so that it is interpreted phonetically in a lower position in TP.

3.3.3 German Long Topicalization

The apparent altruistic addition of P-features to Fin, which allows a phrase to be extracted early from TP, is a signal component in German long topicalization structures, such as the (44) example.

(44) *German* (Salzmann 2005)
Den Maler   glaube ich, mag Petra *t.*
the painter think I   likes Petra
'I think Petra likes the painter.'

In the root clause here, as in the Dutch case just discussed, we may analyze this sentence as one in which addition of a [$\overline{\text{MD}}$] feature to Fin brings the topic to the edge of FinP, from which it is attracted to [Spec, Fin] by the P-feature of Top. In the embedded clause, however, there should be no TopP, since nothing is interpreted as the topic of the embedded clause. Nevertheless, the finite verb raises to Fin in the embedded clause. This apparent verb-first word order makes sense if we consider the structure of the embedded clause before any Ā-movement has taken place:

(45) Fin$^+$ [$_\text{TP}$ Petra den Maler mag-T]

Once again, the topic phrase, *den Maler*, bears an active $_{[\text{TOP}]}$ feature, so Fin will try to attract it if possible. Fin therefore takes on the [$\overline{\text{MD}}$] feature and provokes the topic DP. With merger of *den Maler* in [Spec, Fin], the ϕ-features of Fin can no longer attract the subject *Petra*, so it attracts the finite verb *mag* instead, which then adjoins to Fin. The resulting structure of the complement clause FinP is (46).

(46) [$_\text{FinP}$ den Maler mag-T-Fin [$_\text{TP}$ Petra *t t*]]

Subsequent movement of the topic into higher [Spec, Fin] and [Spec, Top] positions does not affect the position of the finite verb in (46).

3.3.4 Fin and Purely External Matches

Just as T sometimes finds only an external match (see section 2.2), so does Fin. In fact, Fin appears to be able to act both on expletives and on some adverbs in this way. (I assume that adverbs cannot be directly attracted by T for semantic reasons; they cannot appear in an argument position.)

As for Fin finding an external match in adverbs, the evidence comes from comparing root and embedded clauses in the verb-second languages.

In these languages, initial adverbs in root clauses require verb-second structure, but sentential adverbs in embedded clauses can sometimes precede the subject. Consider the contrast in (47).

(47) *Swedish* (Holmberg 1986)
　　a. *Tyvärr　　　Johan inte har läst　denna boken.
　　　　unfortunately Johan not　has read this　　book
　　b. Hon sa　att　tyvärr　　　Johan inte har läst　denna boken.
　　　　She　said that unfortunately Johan not　has read this　　book

The ungrammaticality of (47a) shows that Swedish adverbs like *tyvärr* cannot be adjoined to FinP, or to a higher category in a root clause. While adverbs can certainly appear in [Spec, Top], they can only reach that position if they originate within TP and raise through [Spec, Fin], which produces a structure like:

(48) *Swedish* (Holmberg and Platzack 2005)
　　[$_{TopP}$ Faktiskt Top [$_{FinP}$ *t* hittade-Fin [$_{TP}$ han *e t* pengarna　under
　　　　actually　　　　　　　　found　　　　he　　money-the under
　　sängen.]]]
　　bed-the
　　'Actually he found the money under the bed.'

Notice that movement from inside TP directly to [Spec, Top] must be impossible, too, given the status of (47a).

　　But the acceptability of (47b) cannot arise from movement of the adverb from inside TP, simply because verb-second word order is not triggered. Instead, the adverb in this embedded clause must be merged directly into [Spec, Fin]. We may assume that this is not problematic on semantic grounds; direct insertion of adverbial material into the left periphery is established on other grounds by Rizzi (1990b). The syntactic motivation is what matters here.

　　Since it has already been established that expletives like English *there* can be attracted to [Spec, Fin], we need posit no new resources to say why Fin attracts adverbs, too. It is a short step from locative phrases to adverbs, so let us take it. T and Fin probes can identify phrases with an areal person as matches for their unvalued ϕ-features; they may as well identify adverbs, which can presumably carry equivalent abstract ϕ-features, in the same way. And nothing evidently prevents Fin from seeking its goal in the numeration, rather than in its TP complement. Fin will never attract an adverb from within TP, of course, without triggering verb-second structure, because the subject and T will always be closer matches for Fin within TP than an adverb can be.

The same option of merging adverbs directly into [Spec, Fin] must be available in a root clause, of course. But this does not present any empirical difficulty, since verb-second word order is guaranteed by the dependent nature of Fin in root clauses even when topicalization does not take place.[8] In other words, a structure like (49) is a legitimate alternative to (48), if *faktiskt* is not interpreted as the sentence topic.[9]

(49) [$_{FinP}$ Faktiskt hittade-Fin [$_{TP}$ han pengarna under sängen]]

There is no reason to suppose that the same opportunity for structural ambiguity is absent in English. Consider (50), for example.

(50) a. She said that unfortunately John won't walk the dog.
     b. Unfortunately John won't walk the dog.

Because English does not signal topicalization with verb-second word order, both of the structures in (51) are possible for (50).

(51) a. (She said that) [$_{FinP}$ unfortunately [$_{TP}$ John won't walk the dog.]]
     b. (She said that) [$_{TopP}$ unfortunately [$_{FinP}$ John Fin [$_{TP}$ *t* won't walk the dog.]]]

Data discussed by Vikner (1991) introduces an interesting wrinkle into this picture. In the verb-second Germanic languages generally, it appears that adverbs cannot be merged directly into [Spec, Fin] if there is a pronominal subject in [Spec, T], as illustrated in (52).

(52) *German*
     a. Sie hat gesagt daß vielleicht der Junge sowas getan hat.
         she has said   that maybe   the boy   such done has
     b. *Sie hat gesagt daß vielleicht er sowas getan hat.
         she has said   that maybe   he such done has

(53) *Swedish*
     a. ?Hon sa att tyvärr   Johan inte har läst denna boken.
         he said that unfortunately Johan not has read this book
     b. *Hon sa att tyvärr   han inte har läst denna boken.
         he said that unfortunately he not has read this book

In Icelandic, this peculiar restriction is taken one step further: not only pronouns, but all subjects prevent adverbs from merging directly into [Spec, Fin]. It is tempting to try to connect this difference between Icelandic and Swedish, for example, to another difference between the two language types that involves the distinction between pronouns and DPs. Object shift in Swedish only affects pronouns; in Icelandic, object shift affects objects of any size. It may be, therefore, that subjects that are inclined to move leftward—pronouns in Swedish and German, all DPs in Icelandic—somehow are preferred when Fin is looking for something to provoke. At present, however, I see no way to implement this hunch properly.

It may be relevant that all cases in which an adverb is merged directly into [Spec, Fin] are structures in which an alternative derivation from the same numeration is always possible. Thus in (53a), a grammatical sentence arises if the adverb is merged earlier, by adjoining to auxiliary verb phrase, for example:

(54) ...att   Johan inte tyvärr   har läst denna boken
       that Johan not unfortunately has read this   book

3.3.5 Stylistic T-to-Fin Movement
The status of subject-initial verb-second clauses, like the Dutch (55), is quite different.

(55) Hans heeft dat   boek gelezen.
       Hans has   read this book

Unlike English, Dutch requires T-to-Fin movement even in subject-initial root clauses. This movement cannot be driven by provocative features of Fin—indeed, the P-feature model is designed to ensure that such movement will not be syntactically necessary in sentences like this. The presence of the subject in clause-initial position shows that Fin chooses the subject as its goal for valuing ϕ-features. With the subject then merged into [Spec, Fin], the provocative ϕ-features in Fin have no further role to play in this sentence. Something else must be going on that triggers the verb movement in this case.

Consider what is at stake. It is necessary to say that English and Dutch differ in some way simply in order to achieve descriptive adequacy with respect to sentences like (55). The difference should not, however, be a deep one. Basic principles governing derivations must be identical in both languages. Optimally, in fact, the difference should be quite shallow, involving some small variable property of a single functional category.

Working in an earlier minimalist model of clause structure, Zwart (1993) proposes that Agr$_S$ in Dutch is defective in that it must be attached to a head with lexical content. English, in contrast, has an Agr$_S$ that can stand alone. Adapting this proposal to the current model, we may say that English Fin may stand alone, while Dutch Fin must be attached to another head. In that case, the verb movement in (55) may reflect a repair strategy in which the finite verb raises to Fin simply in order to satisfy the latter's "affixal" requirements. (And the same could then be true of T-to-Fin movement in subject-initial root clauses in other Germanic languages.) We may even suppose that the verb movement in (55) is a stylistic operation, which takes place after all core syntactic operations (within a phase) are finished. The difference between Dutch and English then is minimal, involving the affixal status of Fin.[10]

In fact, two properties set English apart from the other Germanic languages: the affixal status of Fin and the ability of Fin to take on a [$\overline{\text{MD}}$] feature (instead of the [MD] feature alone). This observation suggests that a link might be found that connects these two properties of Fin. Unfortunately, I see no fruitful way at present to undertake this sort of research program. It is not obvious where one would be more likely to find an association, which could arise from the structure of UG, in the course of acquisition, or or simply as a coincidence.

3.4 Conclusion

Since the Government-and-Binding era in generative syntax, the general inclination has been to characterize movement, especially movement to specifier positions, in terms of the result it produces. This made sense in the strongly representational models of the start of this period; it is less clear that it does so today.

If movement involves a copying component at all, then there are two facets to the movement operation: the copying and the placement of the copy. By and large, the literature has treated the latter as the fundamental part of movement, taking the former as a necessary reflex that enables the placement. What I am arguing here is that this conception has things backward. It is really the copying that is fundamental—at least when we are trying to model the mechanism—and the copy placement then takes place automatically.

The case studies examined in this chapter provide empirical justification for reversing the priorities in this way. It is only when we remove the representational constraint—the EPP in whatever form—from our model that the similarities and the competing tensions between specifier movement and head movement start to make sense.

4   Force and Provocation

The idea that movement of heads and phrases is driven by the same mechanism is central to the notion of provocation presented in the preceding two chapters. The uniqueness of the mechanism has perhaps been overlooked in many analyses because independent principles of grammar conspire to make head movement and specifier movement occur in largely complementary environments. In the cases already examined (quotative inversion, verb-second inversion), the significant effects of this premise are seen in contexts where a competition exists between heads and specifiers equidistant to a probe, and where particular circumstances conspire to let the head win the competition. When this combination of events takes place, head movement occurs instead of the expected specifier movement.

There is a second grammatical context where the unity of the mechanism that drives head movement and phrasal movement becomes clear, in which both heads and specifiers can be provoked by the same probe. UG sometimes permits a single feature to trigger movement of multiple items. This phenomenon is well documented in the case of multiple *wh*-movement in Slavic, for example. (See Ura 2000, Richards 1997, and the references cited there.) Given a structure of the form (1), where both XP and YP carry a feature F that matches the unvalued feature on the probe, F may provoke both XP and YP if the language settings permit multiple valuations.

(1)

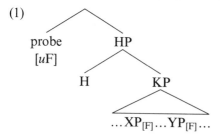

Now suppose the structure in (2), where the unvalued probe feature F matches the corresponding feature on H and XP.

(2)

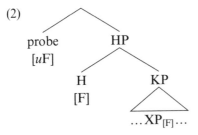

HP cannot be provoked because it is the complement to the probe, but H can be. And once H is attracted to the probe, a subsequent valuation with the same feature can provoke XP. The result of multiple provocations in (2) will be (3):

(3)

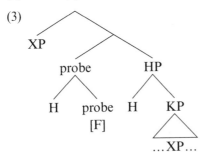

As will be shown, exactly this type of derivation occurs in embedded indirect questions in the "asymmetric" Germanic languages.[1] Many of the otherwise baffling properties of embedded clauses in these languages turn out to receive a quite simple explanation, in fact, once the role played by multiple provocations in their derivation is elucidated.

To be specific, I maintain that an analysis along the following lines should be adopted for a simple embedded question like that in Swedish (4).

(4) *Swedish*

    Jag vet   inte vad Lars sa.

    I   know not what Lars said

On completion of the external merge operations in the embedded clause in (4), the structure of embedded ForceP is (5).

(5)

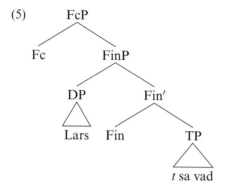

The Force head in (5) contains an unvalued [*u*FORCE] P-feature. Fin contains a valued [FORCE] feature, as does the *wh*-phrase *vad*. *Wh*-movement is driven by provocative [*u*FORCE] features in Force, but the probe cannot access the *wh*-phrase directly, because Fin serves as a closer goal. However, the language allows multiple valuations of [*u*FORCE], so Force can attract both Fin and the *wh*-phrase, which results in structure (6).

(6)

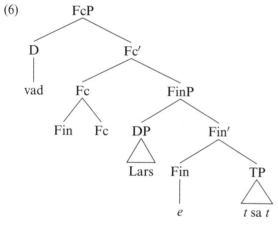

The paired provocation of Fin and a *wh*-phrase does not take place under all circumstances, or in all languages. In the symmetric Germanic languages—Yiddish and Icelandic—Fin does not bear the [FORCE] feature, so it is not provoked by Force. And even in the asymmetric languages, Fin is not provoked if its specifier (the subject) bears a [FORCE] feature and is provoked in its place.

The presence of a [FORCE] feature in Fin is often realized with an overt complementizer (COMP), so that one major difference between symmetric and asymmetric Germanic languages follows from a different base position for the force-marking complementizers.[2] In symmetric languages, complementizers are introduced into the derivation in the Force position; in asymmetric languages, they originate in Fin.

(7) a. *Symmetric force-marking structure*

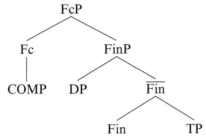

   b. *Asymmetric force-marking structure*

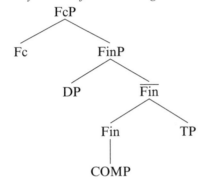

There are thus two allomorphic variants of Fin in declarative clauses in the asymmetric languages: the dependent verbal affix, which is supported by verb raising, as discussed in chapter 2, and the declarative complementizer, which does not need support, but which is interpreted properly only at the edge of the clause (Pesetsky 1998).[3] Complementizers in Fin must therefore raise to Force.

Icelandic and Yiddish make use of the (7a) structures; complementizers in these languages never originate in Fin, so the dependent verbal affix is always present. As a consequence, the finite verb must always raise to Fin in embedded clauses, just as it does in root clauses.[4]

The [FORCE] feature does not compel every head or phrase that bears it to appear at a clause edge. The [FORCE] feature marks phrases as "potential force markers," which can carry a certain interpretation when they introduce a clause, but that may still be interpretable otherwise.

As discussed in section 4.2, operators like interrogative and relative pronouns also bear a [FORCE] feature, which can be attracted by a provocative [uFORCE] feature in Force, forcing *wh*-movement. Questions and relative clauses thus sometimes involve interactions between complementizer attraction and *wh*-movement because a complementizer in Fin, being close to Force, ensures intervention effects on movement of a less local force marker.

The provocative [*u*FORCE] feature can be canceled if there is incorporation of Force by a matrix predicate. When this occurs, asymmetric languages allow embedded verb-second structures.

When Force is missing entirely, symmetric languages and asymmetric languages behave in a similar fashion. Force is always absent in root clauses, because of how phase interpretation is regulated. And in asymmetric languages, Force is sometimes absent in embedded clauses with a missing specifier in FinP, because then the complementizer in Fin need not raise to appear at the edge of its clause.

The evidence for these claims now follows.

4.1 Evidence for Fin-to-Force Movement

4.1.1 Complementizer Agreement

Several dialects of Dutch and German require agreement in number and sometimes in person between a complementizer and the subject of a finite clause (Goeman 1980; Bennis and Haegeman 1984). Examples appear in (8). (The Bavarian examples are taken from Goeman 1980; the Dutch examples, from Zwart 1997.)

(8) a. *Munich Bavarian*
       damid**sd**   net kommsd.
       so-that-2SG not come-2SG
    b. *Brabants*
       dat-**de**   gullie kom-t.
       that-2PL you   come-2PL
    c. *East Netherlandic*
       dat-**e**   wij speul-t
       that-1PL we play-1PL

It has already been established that Fin bears ϕ-features. These features will always have already been valued at the point in the derivation at which Force is added to the clause. That being the case, the simplest way to account for the inflection on complementizers is by supposing that Fin raises to Force, as in (9). When Fin adjoins to Force, the inflectional features borne by Fin will then automatically be available when Force is interpreted at PF.

(9)

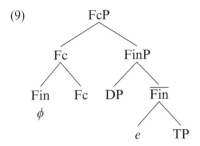

There are other possible approaches, however, that we need to examine to be sure that they cannot succeed. One alternative possibility might be that Force checks ϕ-features on the subject in [Spec, Fin]; another, that Force checks the subject trace within TP. A third way to accommodate the facts would suppose that Force checks ϕ-features on Fin, but without triggering any movement. However, all three of these alternatives face difficulty when the agreement pattern for embedded verb-second clauses is examined. In Dutch and Frisian embedded verb-second clauses, the complementizer remains visible (unlike German), and it precedes the rest of the clause, as usual. But the overt complementizer loses its agreement morphology (DeHaan and Weerman 1986; Zwart 1997). (The data in (10) are attributed by Zwart to Meer 1988.)

(10) a. Heit sei dat-st   do soks   net leauwe moast. (Frisian)
        Dad said that-2SG you such-things not believe must
     b. Heit sei dat/*dat-st do moast soks   net leauwe.
        Dad said that/that-2SG you must such-things not believe

The presence of the *st* suffix in (10a) can be explained under any of the four analyses suggested above. If Fin raises to Force, then it brings its ϕ-features along with it, which may then have a morphological reflex. If Force is valued by ϕ-features on Fin—with or without movement—and Fin agrees with the subject, then ϕ-features can be realized on Force. If instead, Force is valued by ϕ-features on the subject *do*, or its trace in [Spec, T], then again these features can be realized on the subject.

But explaining the absence of agreement in (10b) is a harder task. Suppose the structure of the complement clause in (10b) to be more or less (11), with the categories left open for the verb-second portion of the clause, headed by some category F.

(11) ... [FcP dat [do moast-F [*t* soks net leauwe moast]]]

If F bears ϕ-features, then Force should be able to agree with it. Similarly, if [Spec, F] has ϕ-features—and it is difficult to see why it would not—then it should be a suitable goal for the Force probe. And if neither F nor its specifier has accessible ϕ-features, perhaps because such features are not used in the Ā system (contra Branigan and MacKenzie 2002), then the trace of the subject will simply be the closest element that contains ϕ-features and Force should be able to ignore the specifier and head of FP and value its features with the trace. But none of these possibilities can be allowed.

On the other hand, if Force has provoked Fin when complementizer agreement takes place, and if F is Fin in (11), then it is clear why complementizer agreement is impossible here. The word order shows that Fin has not raised to Force; Fin is where the finite verb ends up instead. So Fin cannot have been provoked by Force, which means that agreement cannot be realized.

Similar conclusions can be drawn from considering the effect of preposed adverbs on complementizer agreement. Van Craenenbroeck and Van Koppen (2002) observe that complementizer agreement disappears when an adverb precedes the subject:

(12) *Hellendorn Dutch* (van Craenenbroeck and van Koppen 2002)
    a. *darr-e allichte   wiej de wedstrijd winnen zölt
        that-PL probably we the game   win   will
    b. dat allichte   wiej de wedstrijd winnen zölt
        that probably we the game   win   will
        'that we will probably win the game'

Assuming that the adverb in such cases occupies a [Spec, Top] position, this effect falls together with other head-movement constraint cases as a side effect of provocation. Suppose (12a) has the structure (13) at some point, with complementizer agreement originating in Fin.

(13) [$_{FcP}$ Fc [$_{TopP}$ allichte Top]$_{FinP}$ wiej Fin [$_{TP}$ ... de wedstrijd winnen zölt]]]]

In (13), if Force provokes Fin, the result cannot be that a copy of Fin alone is generated, since FinP is not the complement of Force. Instead, a copy would have to be made of FinP, with the copy then merged at the root. Instead of complementizer agreement, the result would be fronting of FinP past the adverb, with Fin itself remaining in a position to the right of the subject.

Compare the alternatives. If complementizer agreement simply involves a valuation operation that associates Force with the subject, or with Fin in situ, then the presence of an adverb should make no difference.

4.1.2 Asymmetric Provocation of Fin

As a fortuitous side effect of the attraction of Fin by Force in Dutch and Frisian, Fin will be attached to a head with lexical content, which satisfies its own morphological needs. In fact, in non-verb-second embedded clauses generally, the lexical support for Fin may come from the higher Force head that attracts it. No stylistic verb movement to Fin is then motivated (and none occurs). (In root clauses, of course, the Force complementizer is silent or absent, and cannot attract Fin. In root clauses, the stylistic operation discussed in section 3.3.5 is the only way available to support affixal Fin.) And although there is no complementizer agreement morphology to show this, the null hypothesis would seem to be that the same is true of embedded clauses in other Germanic verb-second languages. In embedded clauses in general in these languages, Fin will be supported by the Force head that provokes it.

This approach to embedded clause structure provides an immediate account of the embedded verb-second structures found in Dutch "asymmetric coordination" (Hoekstra 1994).[5]

(14) *Dutch* (Hoekstra 1994, 288, 295)
    a. Het irriteert ons dat je te   laat thuiskomt en je   hebt
       it   irritates us that you too late home-come and you have
       geen sleutel bij   je.
       no   key   with you
    b. als je te laat thuiskomt en je   hebt geen geld   bij
       if you too late home-come and you have no   money with
       je,   dan
       you, then

In this construction, the first of two conjoined clauses is verb-final, while the second has the verb in second position. This construction is particularly noteworthy because it produces verb-second word order in a syntactic context that would normally exclude embedded verb-second clauses in Dutch. So in (14b), for example, the verb-second conjunct is part of a conditional clause. Were the conditional not a coordinate structure, of course, verb-second word order would be impossible, as in (15).

(15) *als je   hebt geen geld   bij je,   dan
     if you have no   money with you, then

What makes this construction possible is the acceptability in Dutch of violations of the Coordinate Structure Constraint in which the first of two conjuncts contains a feature that is accessed by an external probe, without the second conjunct participating in the valuation. This exceptional property of the language is evident from the existence of asymmetric complementizer agreement, observed by van Koppen (2005). In Tegelen Dutch, she shows, second-person singular agreement morphology may appear on the complementizer if the first conjunct in a subject DP is the second singular pronoun.

(16) *Tegelen Dutch* (Van Koppen 2005)
...de-s doow en ich ôs treff-e
that-2SG [youSG and I]1P.PL each.other1P.PL meet-PL
'...that you and I will meet'

Such violations are allowed with cliticization as well.

(17) *Dutch* (Hoekstra 1994)
omdat-tie zich vergist en zijn bror ziek is
because-he himself mistakes and his brother ill is
'because he is mistaken and his brother is ill'

Assuming what is conjoined is some clausal constituent in the domain of the *omdat* complementizer, the clitic subject *ie* in the first conjunct is raised without any parallel movement from within the second conjunct in (17).

Similarly, in the examples of (14), the provocative [FORCE] feature of Force matches Fin, and ensures an external copy will be merged, but only if it matches in the first conjunct. The effect is that a copy of only the first Fin then adjoins to Force. This satisfies the affixal and checking requirements of both Force and the first Fin. The Fin in the second conjunct is left inside its own clause, in a position where support can be found only if the verb raises (stylistically) to Fin.

(18) Het irriteert ons [$_{FcP}$ dat-Fc
[$_{FinP}$ je e [$_{TP}$ t te laat thuiskomt]] en
[$_{Finp}$ je hebt-Fin [$_{TP}$ t geen sleutel bij je e]]]

Notice that Fin in the first conjunct is a component of the *dat* complementizer, while Fin in the second is the verbal affixal variant. This need not be stipulated. As long as Fin may optionally hold either form, the right variants will be forced in these contexts by general principles.

The more usual symmetric coordination pattern is possible as well, as Hoekstra notes.

(19) *Dutch*
Als je te laat thuis komt en je geen geld bij je hebt
if you too late home come and you no money with you have

Here, of course, we may suppose that the provocative [FORCE] feature in Force matches across the board into both conjuncts, as in (20).

(20) [FcP Als [FinP je Fin [TP *t* te laat thuis komt]]

en

[FinP je Fin [TP *t* geen geld bij je hebt]]]]

Fin

Adjunction of Fin to Force then makes verb movement to Fin unnecessary in both clauses.

4.1.3   Overt Manifestations

Although there is clear evidence that Fin moves to Force, this evidence does not itself show exactly what originates in Fin. One possibility, which I have tacitly assumed up to this point, is that Fin always contains the affix that obtains verbal support in verb-second structures. In that case, adjunction of Fin to Force would need to accomplish the same morphological result as adjunction of T to Fin; it would provide a root supporting affixal Fin.[6] This may be possible, but the fact that the relevant complex heads are formed in entirely different ways suggests that we should be cautious in admitting this possibility. Roberts (2001) suggests another line of analysis, which avoids this problem.[7] His idea is that in some languages, the complementizer itself originates in Fin. In that case, in Dutch the complementizer may be merged in its base position with all its (unvalued) agreement morphology present from the start. For example, FinP in the Brabants Dutch example (8b) would have the structure prior to merger with Force under this approach.

(21) [FinP gullie dat-de [TP *t* kom-t]]

The idea that some complementizers originate in Fin offers an explanation for constructions in which multiple "complementizers" are pronounced in the same clause, which is possible in Dutch.

(22) *Dutch* (Zwart 1997)
      a. Piet vroeg of/ofdat Jan   Marie kuste.
          Pete asked if/ifthat John Mary kissed
          'Pete asked whether John kissed Mary.'
      b. Ik weet   niet wie of/ofdat   Marie gekust heeft.
          I   know not who if/ifthat/that Mary kissed has
          'I don't know who Mary kissed.'

The *ofdat* form is clearly a combination of interrogative *of* and declarative *dat*, either of which can be used in isolation in the right type of complement clause. It is surprising, however, that both of them might appear together in a single head position. But suppose that only *of* is a true token of the Force category, and that *dat* originates instead in Fin. Then the earlier structure for the acceptable forms of the complement clause in (22b) is (23).

(23) [FcP of [FinP Jan dat [TP *t* Marie kuste]]]

When Fin raises to Force, the structure (24) is created, and some phonetic interpretation must be arranged for the newly complex Force head.

(24)

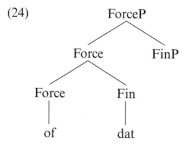

Spell-Out apparently has some flexibility in interpreting this structure in Dutch. It may interpret *of* by itself, deleting *dat*, or it may interpret both units together, to produce the *ofdat* forms.

Notice that no new explanation is necessary for the ungrammaticality of sentences like (25), even if Fin is not always affixal. In embedded clauses of this type, Force still provokes Fin, so *dat* will have to raise from its original position anyway. The ungrammaticality is doubly ensured if *dat* cannot be used in situ together with an overt specifier for FinP.[8]

(25) *Ik denk Jan dat Marie gekust heeft.
        I think Jan that Marie kissed has

To summarize, in some Germanic languages, there is compelling evidence that Force attracts Fin. The declarative complementizer originates in Fin, and Fin-to-Force movement places it at the edge of its clause.

As for the broader question of why Fin-to-Force movement occurs, I assume that this movement is driven by the same formal requirements as T-to-Fin operations. In other words, Force has an unvalued P-feature that matches a feature of Fin. And given that Fin appears to be the original position of declarative complementizers—at least in some languages—a reasonable hypothesis is that Force must value a COMP feature. Given that complementizers signify the clausal force in embedded clauses, the most likely candidate for a feature that connects Fin and Force is a [FORCE] feature, which is unvalued in Force and valued in Fin.

Beyond the formal mechanism, there may be interpretive exigencies that encourage Fin-to-Force movement. Force markers normally appear at the edge of their clause; it appears that this is where clausal force should be signified. Pesetsky (1998) suggests that the "doubly filled Comp" effect might be derived from the need for C to appear at the left edge of its clause. A slight variation on Pesetsky's proposal would be to say that *force markers* must be found at the edge of their clauses in order to be interpreted as such. If so, then a force marker that originates in Fin will have to be attracted by Force and the provocative [*u*FORCE] feature of Force simply provides the necessary opportunity.[9]

In English too, declarative complementizers seem to originate in Fin— most of the time, anyway. So a sentence like (26) will have the structure indicated, with *that* attracted from Fin to adjoin to Force.

(26) I believe [$_{FcP}$ [$_{Fc}$ that-Fc] [$_{FinP}$ children e [$_{TP}$ t are our future]]].

When topicalization occurs, though, Fin-to-Force movement is impossible. (See section 4.3 for discussion of this point.) So in sentences like (27), and in embedded negative inversion examples like (28), the complementizer must originate in Force; Fin must be the silent head found in root clauses for these structures.

(27) I think that tomorrow you should get the car fixed.

(28) Pam said that never could she fire a Haligonian.

In English, then, there are two positions in which complementizers may originate: Force and Fin.

English data that supports this analysis is highly variable, both dialectally and in the strength of individual speaker judgments. One type of evidence is presented by McCloskey (2007), who notes the frequency in English of sentences in which a *that* complementizer appears twice in a single embedded clause. Some of McCloskey's examples appear in (29).

(29) a. But the simple analysis which suggests that because American investment takes place here that we should be a lapdog for their efforts in the war is one that I think is quite objectionable and quite offensive.

   b. He thinks that if you are in a bilingual classroom that you will not be encouraged to learn English.

   c. My fervent prayer is that for the sake of the president and the sake of this nation that this matter is resolved soon.

   d. I don't think that he should contend that just because he makes a promise that it becomes a responsibility of the United States.

Clauses in which doubled *that* appear tend to be long and complex, and the two instances of *that* must be separated by a lengthy conditional clause or other long topic. To me, these sentences feel like performance errors, but I am confident that they are actually grammatical for some speakers. In any case, the fact that the complementizer can appear in two distinct positions at all supports the idea that in less wordy embedded clauses, the complementizer is still associated with two positions in an abstract sense.

Let us examine the relevant portion of (29a) more closely:

(30) ... suggests [that because American investment takes place here that we should be a lapdog for their efforts in the war] ...

Within the complement clause in (30), there is a second topicalized embedded clause *because American investment takes place here*. If we assume that this is located in the usual topic position of [Spec, Top], then one overt complementizer is inside TopP and one is outside it. The natural conclusion is that the former appears in Fin and the latter, in Force. A fuller picture of (30) is then the structure in (31).

(31) ... suggests [$_{FcP}$ that [$_{TopP}$ [because American investment takes place here] [$_{FinP}$ that [$_{TP}$ we should be a lapdog...]]]] ...

Compare this structure with that of the simpler complement clause having single complementizer in (32).

(32) The evidence suggests [$_{FcP}$ that [$_{TopP}$ [when sentences get long] [$_{FinP}$ people [$_{Fin}$ ∅] [$_{TP}$ *t* are likely to get lost]]]].

The structures differ in two ways. The Fin position is occupied by different material: *that* versus a zero form. The use of *that* in a position that is not at the clause edge is the surprising property of (31), since *that* should be interpreted as a force marker. It may be that the size of the preceding topicalized clause makes FinP count as something more like a complete clause; it is immediately preceded by the right edge of another embedded clause, after all. Another possibility might be that *that* really does move to Force in (31), but that the trace retains its phonetic content because of the locality violation involved in skipping past the intervening Top head.

The other difference between the two structures is that [Spec, Fin] contains the subject in (32), but not in (31). The provocative ϕ-features in Fin should compel the subject to raise in both sentences. Again, the failure of provocation in (30) may make the sentence more acceptable because the subject does not occupy the edge position in FinP, so that *that*–in situ is less problematic. For speakers for whom the (29) sentences are truly grammatical, though, this pattern must signal dialectal variation in whether Fin bears P-features at all. It looks as if some dialects do permit Fin to lack P-features in some contexts. (This turns out to be possible in specific contexts in some dialects of Scandinavian, too. See section 5.3 for discussion.)

Of course, in a language in which complementizers always originate in Force, there will be no need for further movement, and Fin will then presumably lack [FORCE] features altogether. As will be seen, this is the situation in Icelandic and Yiddish.

4.2 On *Wh*-Movement

4.2.1 Force in Embedded Questions

In *wh*-questions (in languages with overt *wh*-movement), the force-marking information is supplied not primarily by the complementizer, but by the fronted *wh*-phrase in [Spec, Force]. If the [FORCE] feature means what the label implies, then [FORCE] should be a property of *wh*-phrases, too. If we consider the use of [FORCE] in terms of its expressive function, it would be preferable in questions for Force to attract a *wh*-phrase instead of a Fin complementizer. But formal considerations prevent this from taking place, except in questions in which the *wh*-phrase is the subject. And the formal limits imposed by Universal Grammar turn out to produce quite intricate surface effects in the syntax of embedded questions.

Consider the Dutch embedded question in (33).

(33) *Dutch* (Koster 1987)
    Ik vraag me af waar hij *t* onder door   ging.
    I wonder   where he   under through went

Force attracts *waar* to [Spec, Force]. The usual assumption is that it does so to check a [WH] feature, but the label of the provocative feature is simply a matter of nomenclature. We can achieve the same empirical result—Ā movement of a *wh*-phrase—if Force can attract *waar* with a [FORCE] feature. And since we have already seen evidence that Force attracts other force markers, it seems more economical to suppose that the same type of feature drives movement in *wh*-questions.

There is a complication, though. Since Fin bears a value for the [FORCE] feature in Dutch, the closest match for [*u*FORCE] in Force will normally be Fin, even in questions. If *wh*-movement is driven by this feature, the process will have to involve multiple provocations by [*u*FORCE], or multiple [*u*FORCE] features associated with the Force head. In any case, the first provocation will necessarily attract Fin to Force. Only afterward can a second provocation look further into the clause to attract a *wh*-phrase upward. So the embedded clause in (33) ends up with the structure (34) after both Fin and the *wh*-phrase are provoked by Force.

(34) [FcP waar Fc-Fin [FinP hij *e* [TP *t t* onder door ging]]]

For questions in which the *wh*-phrase is the subject, the presence of [*u*FORCE] in Force will have a different effect. Consider (35).

(35) *Dutch* (Koster 1987, 207)
  Ik weet   niet wie of (dat) *t* het gedaan heeft.
  I know not who if that   it   done   has
  'I do not know who did it.'

The *wh*-phrase *wie* must occupy [Spec, Fin] at a certain point in the derivation, because Fin has provocative ϕ-features that attract the subject. Therefore, the structure in which the [FORCE] feature of Force seeks a match is (36).

(36)

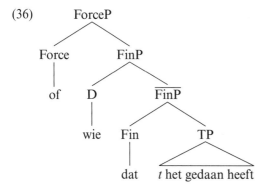

Both *dat* and *wie* are accessible to the [*u*FORCE] feature of Force. They are equidistant, in fact. But specifier attraction is preferred to head attraction, so *of* attracts only *wie* in (36). The complementizer *dat* in Fin remains in situ. But this is evidently not problematic in Dutch, where overt complementizers are permissible even when not interpreted as force markers.

Data uncovered in Taraldson's (1986a) description of embedded questions in Norwegian confirms the difference in complementizer positions in subject and nonsubject *wh*-questions. In Norwegian, the *som* complementizer appears obligatorily with a local subject *wh*-phrase; see (37).

(37) *Norwegian* (Taraldsen 1986a)
     Vi vet   hvem *(som) snakker med Marit.
     we know who   talks   with Mary

Swedish behaves like Norwegian in this respect.

The appearance of *som* in such embedded questions is initially quite surprising, given that Norwegian is otherwise sensitive to doubly filled Comp effects, even in cases where *som* is involved, as in the relative clause in (38).

(38) Her er mannen hvis   hest   (*som) vant låpet.
     here is the-man whose horse   won the-race

These peculiar properties of *som* in embedded subject questions indicate that *som* in (37) does not appear in the Force position. If *som* occupies Fin, then the absence of a doubly filled Comp effect follows, simply because there is no overt head in Force to clash with the overt *wh*-phrase specifier. And if *som* remains in Fin, then it must be overt because there is no specifier present to induce silence.

The structure of the embedded question in (37) then must be (39).

(39) [$_{FcP}$ hvem [$_{Fc}$ $\emptyset$] [$_{FinP}$ t som [$_{TP}$ t snakker med Marit]]]

Recall that Force normally attracts Fin, including *som*, and that this is why the finite verb does not have to raise to Fin in embedded clauses in verb-second languages. Force must therefore have a provocative feature that checks Fin. In (39), though, *som* does not raise. In this structure, then, Force must be checking the relevant feature by attracting the subject *hvem* to Spec-Fc instead.

This structure, in which the *wh*-phrase and *som* appear in different projections, is supported by the fact that *som* can be further separated from its *wh*-phrase by right dislocation in Swedish (Holmberg 1986).

(40) Jag vet   vilka fotbollslag,   och Peter vet   vilka hästar som
     I   know which football teams and Peter knows which horses
     kommer att vinna den här veckan.
     will   win   this   week

In (40), the right-dislocated phrase is FinP, which contains *som* and out of which the subject *wh*-phrases have raised to become specifiers for ForceP.

It is impossible, in fact, to leave *som* behind and dislocate a bare TP (Platzack 1986). In this respect *som* is more closely bound to TP than an argumental *att* complementizer is. (Examples are taken from Platzack 1986.)

(41) a. *Jag vet   vilka fotbollslag som, och Peter vet   vilka
          I   know which soccer team   and Peter knows which
          hästar som kommer att vinna den här veckan.
          horses   come   to win   this   week
      b. Jag tror   att, men vet   inte säkert om,   din   teori
          I   believe that, but know not for sure whether your theory
          är korrekt.
          is correct

The difference between *som* and *att* follows from the principles that influence provocation. In each of the complement clauses in (41), the [uFORCE] feature of Force must provoke something. In (41a), it has access to both Fin and the *wh*-phrase in [Spec, Fin], so it chooses the latter, because specifier attraction is preferable to head attraction. In (41b), however, the only available match for the [uFORCE] feature of Force is Fin, so Fin gets raised.

In embedded questions where the *wh*-phrase is not the subject, *som* is obligatorily absent in Norwegian.

(42) *Norwegian* (Taraldsen 1986a)
      *Ve vet   hvem som Marit snakker med.
       we know who   Marit talks   with

This is to be expected, since Fin raises to Force in such questions. Force must provoke the closest element bearing [FORCE] before it can provoke a more distant element, so it attracts Fin before it can attract the *wh*-phrase. In (42), *som* would have raised to Force, and the ungrammaticality reflects the requirement in this language that nothing be pronounced in the Force position when there is a specifier. In other words, this is a run-of-the-mill doubly filled Comp effect.

Although Swedish patterns with Norwegian in requiring *som* in embedded subject *wh*-questions, it differs slightly in what is permitted in other *wh*-questions.

(43) *Swedish* (Platzack 1986)
      Jag undrar vem (som) Sara kommer att träffa på festen.
       I   wonder who   Sara come   to meet at the-party

Som is optional in such cases.[10] This evidently superficial difference between Norwegian and Swedish can be attributed to differences in how structure (44) is interpreted at PF.

(44)

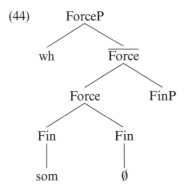

In Norwegian, as we have seen, the doubly filled Comp effect applies absolutely in this structure, so that *som* cannot be pronounced. In Swedish, the PF interpretation is more flexible, and either *som* or the empty Force head are allowed to be pronounced, despite the presence of the specifier. In both languages, though, *som* must be pronounced when it remains in Fin and its specifier is raised.

In German, where Fin also hosts the declarative complementizer, Force will bear an inherent [*u*FORCE] feature. And the effects are similar to what we have seen in Dutch and Swedish. The complementizer is optionally pronounced.

(45) *German* (Müller 1995)
     Ich weiß nicht wen (daß) du gesehen hast.
     I   know knot who that you seen   have

In Icelandic, the symmetric Scandinavian language, *sem*—the Icelandic counterpart to *som*—cannot appear in Fin at all, because such languages require that complementizers always originate in Force. We therefore do not expect to find *sem* in structures where Force is not expressed. And this prediction is confirmed in (46).

(46) *Icelandic* (Platzack 1986)
     a. Hún spurði hver hefði keypt   bókina.
        she   asked   who had   bought the-book
     b. Hún spurði hvað hann hefði keypt.
        she   asked   what he   had   bought

Yiddish, the symmetric West Germanic language, also lacks complementizers in Fin. We expect not to see doubly filled Comp violations in this language, which appears to be the case.

(47) *Yiddish* (Diesing 1990)

Ikh veys nit vuhin ir geyt.

I know not where you go

Because Fin lacks a [FORCE] feature in Yiddish, interrogative Force may simply attract *wh*-phrases directly from their TP-internal position.

English embedded questions work like their Dutch or Swedish counterparts. Force in questions also bears a [*u*FORCE] P-feature, so it will attract something. The presence of a [FORCE] feature in English Fin means that Fin must always be attracted first when nonsubject *wh*-movement occurs in English embedded questions. The complement clause in (48) thus has the structure indicated.

(48) Pam asked [$_{FcP}$ which truck Fin-Fc [$_{FinP}$ Jerry *e* [$_{TP}$ *t* wore out the clutch on *t*]]]

This difference between subject and nonsubject *wh*-movement is responsible for the asymmetries in (49).

(49) a. I wonder who *t* likes Jan and *t* impresses Sue.
b. I wonder who Jan likes *t* and Sue counts on *t*.
c. *I wonder who Jan likes *t* and *t* impresses Sue.
d. *I wonder who *t* likes Jan and Sue impresses *t*.

These data are the second half of the cases discussed by Williams (1978), who shows that subjects cannot be extracted "across the board" together with nonsubjects. Only local extraction of subjects is constrained in this manner. When subjects are extracted from an embedded clause, they may be extracted in parallel with a nonsubject.

(50) a. I wonder who Jan likes *t* and Sue believes/wants *t* to be dependable.
b. ?I wonder who Jan likes *t* and Sue thinks *t* is dependable.
c. I wonder who Sue thinks *t* is dependable and Jan likes *t*.

The acceptability of (50c) shows that the issue is not one of Case conflict, since *who* comes from a nominative source in one clause and an accusative source in the other. Instead, the problem has to do with the derivation of embedded *wh*-questions. Fin must raise to Force to attract nonsubjects, but Fin does not raise when local subjects are attracted. In (49d), for example, the first and only thing provoked by Force in the first conjunct is the *wh*-phrase *who*, but the closest match for [*u*FORCE] in the second conjunct is Fin. There is no way to provoke *who* and Fin together in across-the-board fashion, because they are completely different. Therefore,

extraction constitutes a violation of the coordinate structure constraint.
And the same is true of (49c).

4.2.2 Force in Relative Clauses

Like embedded questions, relative clauses generally employ a Force head
with a P-feature to attract the relative pronoun to the [Spec, Force] position. Force in relative clauses also attracts Fin with a provocative [FORCE]
feature, at least in the languages where it does so in other clause types.
Example (51) is a typical structure, then, with OP indicating the silent relative pronoun.[11]

(51) the tent

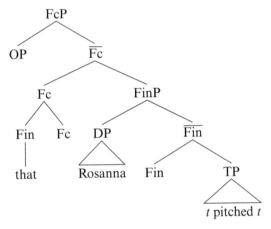

The most interesting issues in the analysis of relative clauses are found
in the analysis of subject relatives, which are often different from the rest.
In some languages, subject relatives make use of a distinct complementizer, or of a complementizer that behaves in unexpected ways. The
French relative complementizer *qui*, for example, appears only with subject relative pronouns (Kayne 1972). And Swedish/Norwegian *som* is optional for nonsubject relative clauses, but obligatory in subject relatives.
The same is true of English *that*.

(52) *French*
    le   gars qui est arrivé   hier
    the guy that is arrived yesterday
    'the guy that arrived yesterday'

(53) *Swedish*
    a. mannen *(som) pratar med Johann
       the-man that   talks with Johann

b. mannen (som) vi pratar med
   the-man that   we talk   with

(54) the man *(that) arrived yesterday

Complementizers themselves should not be sensitive to the grammatical function of phrases they attract, so the literature has had difficulty accommodating data like this. In the P-model, though, these facts fall into place quickly. As in questions, Force in relative clauses attracts the closest element bearing [FORCE], and then it continues to attract more distant [FORCE]-bearing elements if necessary. In Norwegian and Swedish, *som*, which originates in Fin, bears [FORCE] and so does the silent relative pronoun. If the relative pronoun is the subject, then the ϕ^+ features of *som* attract it to [Spec, Fin], so Force attracts the relative pronoun directly. If the relative pronoun is not the subject, then Force must attract *som* first, before it can engage in secondary provocation with the more distant relative pronoun.

The existence of some doubly filled Comp effects in relative clauses presents a complication, however. Recall from the discussion of Norwegian *som* in indirect questions that *som* is audible in questions because it does not appear in the same phrase as a subject *wh*-phrase; *som* remains in Fin, while the *wh*-phrase raises to [Spec, Force]. But in relative clauses, doubly filled Comp effects do interfere with pronounciation of *som*, as in (38), repeated.

(38) Her er mannen hvis   hest   (*som) vant låpet.
      here is the-man whose horse   won the-race

The unacceptability of *som* with *hvis hest* makes sense only if the relative phrase occupies [Spec, Fin], and not [Spec, Force]. This means that relative clause structure will not always be identical to that of embedded questions. Unlike questions, relative clauses need not always be full ForceP categories. Instead, they may consist of smaller FinP clauses. The structure of the (grammatical) DP in (38) must therefore be (55).

(55)

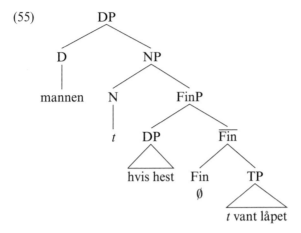

The reason for the reduced structure in subject relatives (compared to embedded subject questions) is presumably that the Force category is superfluous in relatives. While Force in questions is part of what identifies them as interrogative, Force in a relative clause adds no information that cannot be deduced from the context. In nonsubject relative clauses, ForceP must be present to make A-bar movement of the relative pronoun possible, and without A-bar movement, the requisite operator-variable chain does not arise. But subjects are attracted to [Spec, Fin] in any case, so FinP is adequate to all the interpretational demands of a subject relative. In practice, this implies that relative clauses will be FinP only when the subject is the relative pronoun; with other relative pronouns, Ā movement must involve provocation by the [uFORCE] feature of Force.

(56) a. *Subject relatives*

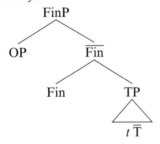

b. *Nonsubject relatives*

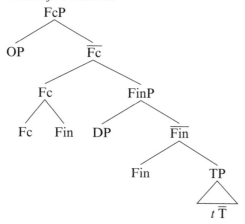

Examples like French (52) and Swedish (53a) are then cases in which a bare FinP serves as the relative clause, and in which the Fin head, *qui* or *som*, remains visible because it does not raise to a higher Force. *Qui*, like *som*, is how Fin sounds when not adjoined to Force.[12]

The English facts are hardly more complicated. Like *qui* and *som*, English relative *that* seems to be sensitive to the grammatical function of the null relative pronoun. While *that* can be omitted with nonsubject relative pronouns, it cannot with subject relative pronouns:

(57) a.   the chair (that) we bought
     b.   the couch (that) we sat on
     c.   *the bear *(that) chased us

It is easy enough to accommodate this data now. Like Swedish and French, English relative clauses may be either full ForceP categories or reduced FinPs. The latter is possible, again, only when the relative pronoun is the subject in [Spec, Fin], because otherwise movement of the relative pronoun out of TP could not take place. So the relative clause is ForceP in (57a) and (57b), but FinP in (57c). In (57c), the complementizer *that* must occupy Fin, and it is obligatorily pronounced (when the specifier is null). The derivation of ForceP in (57a) and (57b) is more involved. Suppose the structure of ForceP in (57a) to be (58), prior to any provocation by Force, with OP representing the null relative pronoun.

(58)

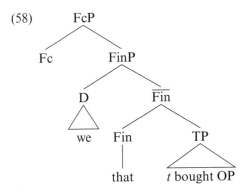

Recall that English Fin bears a [FORCE] feature, even though Force need not bear [*u*FORCE]. If Force does bear [*u*FORCE], which it must do in order to trigger *wh*-movement, then it must provoke Fin before it can provoke the relative pronoun. The resulting structure must then be (59).

(59)

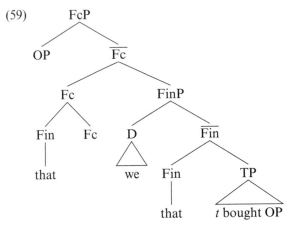

There have to be two options for realizing the complex head now occupying Force. Either *that* is pronounced, or the null Force head is pronounced. This is entirely analogous to what we have already seen with Swedish *som*.

This treatment of subject relative clauses offers a principled account of one variety of so-called vacuous movement effects. Chung and McCloskey (1983) observe that relative clauses formed by subject extraction are weaker extraction islands than relative clauses formed by extraction of any other type of argument. Examples (from Chung and McCloskey 1983) appear in (60a).

(60) a. That's one trick that I've known a lot of people who've been taken in by *t*.

b. Isn't that the song that Paul and Stevie were the only ones who wanted to record *t*?

Such sentences compare favorably with sentences in which the operator comes from somewhere else, as in (61).

(61) ??Isn't that the song writer that ballads were the only things that Paul would write *t* for *t*?

In indirect questions, the contrast is absent.[13]

As Chung and McCloskey (1983) argue, this contrast is best explained if subjects and nonsubjects appear in different positions. For them, the subject occupies a different position because it does not move from its TP-internal position at all. But a less ad hoc treatment is possible in the present model. Since subject relative pronouns do not raise higher than Spec-FinP, it is possible to find an escape hatch for nonsubjects in these cases. Suppose that early in the derivation, the structure of the relevant DP in (60a) is (62):

(62) [$_{DP}$ people [$_{FinP}$ who$_i$ Fin lbTP t_i have been taken in by which]]]

The bare FinP in (62) is a legitimate relative clause because it contains a relative pronoun that has undergone Ā movement. To escape from DP, then, the *wh*-phrase *which* must find a way out of FinP, but there is no ForceP phase to block movement, so movement is unobstructed.

In contrast, the structure of the island DP in (61) can only be (63).

(63) [$_{DP}$ the only things [$_{FcP}$ $_j$ OP that [$_{FinP}$ Paul$_i$ [$_{TP}$ t_i would write t_j for whom]]]]

Here there is no escape hatch available for the relative pronoun *whom*. Spec-ForceP is already occupied, so *whom* can only escape from the relative clause by violating the *Phase Impenetrability Condition*.

Another circumstance in which bare FinP appears to be acceptable is in some conditional clauses. Conditional clauses headed by *if* complementizers are simply ForceP categories with a particular head, which suits their semantic function. As usual, we can assume that *if* carries a provocative [FORCE] feature, so that Fin must raise and adjoin to *if* in (64a).

(64) a. If a picture paints a thousand words, then I should just make pictures.
    b. Were a picture good enough, I could stop writing this.

There is no visible complementizer in (64b), though, and the word order shows that T raises to Fin in this case, leaving the subject in [Spec, T].

Suppose that Germanic conditional clauses may make use of a null conditional operator, similar to Larson's (1985) null *whether*. If the null conditional operator raises to [Spec, Fin], then the ϕ-features of Fin will have to provoke T and the the subject in TP, so that the auxiliary movement to Fin is forced. And null FinP will be permitted in this situation because Fin appears at the edge of FinP, the specifier for FinP being silent. The full structure for (64b) is then what we see in (65).

(65) [TopP [FinP Ø were [TP a picture *e t* good enough]] [FinP I Fin [TP *t* could stop writing this]]]

The notorious *da/die* alternation in West Flemish relative clauses (Bennis and Haegeman 1984) presents a slightly different challenge. The regular pattern for complementizers in this language is seen in (66) and (67).

(66) *W. Flemish* (Bennis and Haegeman 1984)
      Wien peinst Pol da   *t* Valère gezien heet?
      who thinks Pol that   Valère seen   has
      'Who does Pol think Valère has seen?'

(67) a. den vent da/*die   Pol getrokken heet
         the man that/who Pol painted   has
         'the man who Pol made a picture of'
     b. den vent da/die   gekommen is
         the man that/who come   is

In simple declarative complements, with or without long extraction, the agreeing complementizer *da* is used. In relative clauses where the subject provides the gap, either *da* or the relative pronoun *die* may appear. With other types of relative clauses, *die* is unacceptable, and only the *da* complementizer may appear.

The restriction of *die* to subject relatives alone patterns with Norwegian *som*, and can be analyzed along the same lines. In asymmetric verb-second languages like this, the complementizer originates in Fin, and not in Force. Usually, though, the [uFORCE] feature of Force provokes Fin, which then raises upward. The complementizer *da* appears when Force provokes Fin in this way. *Da* may be taken to be the PF interpretation of the structure in which Fin is adjoined to Force in West Flemish.

With subject relative clauses, the (null) subject relative pronoun is provoked by Force instead, so Fin remains in its original location. *Die* is then what the complementizer sounds like when it is not raised to Force, which occurs when only FinP is projected in the relative clause.

The optional use of *da* in subject relatives remains to be explained. But Bennis and Haegeman (1984) show that subjects may freely occur postverbally in *da* clauses. With Taraldsen (1986a), I suppose that this accounts for the appearance of *da* where one would otherwise expect *die*. If the relative pronoun occupies a position other than [Spec, T] before undergoing Ā movement, then it will not be attracted to [Spec, Fin]. Presumably, [Spec, T] is occupied by an expletive that raises to [Spec, Fin] in its place. But then Force cannot provoke the subject relative pronoun directly, but must first provoke the closer Fin. So Fin adjoins to Force when the subject relative pronouns is "inverted" in TP, and the Fin-Force head is interpreted as *da* in the usual way.

In Icelandic and Yiddish, both subject and nonsubject relative clauses will necessarily be full ForceP phrases. In the Icelandic (68) examples, *sem* originates in Force, and it does not attract Fin. It does, however, attract the silent subject relative pronoun from [Spec, Fin], by provoking the closest phrase with a [*u*FORCE] feature.

(68) a. *Icelandic* (Holmberg 2000)
    Þeir   sem hafa verið í Ósló segja að
    those   have been in Oslo say   that
   b. (Sigurdhsson 1997)
    Þeir   sem verða að taka þessa erfiðu   ákvörðun
    those   have   taken this difficult decision

4.3   The Distribution of Embedded Verb-Second Clauses

Provocation of [FORCE] by Force is fundamental to the properties of regular embedded clauses, and in the asymmetric Germanic languages, this operation triggers both head movement and phrasal movement. Under certain circumstances, however, the ability of Force to provoke is *canceled*. The prediction made by a provocation model is that both head movement (of Fin) and phrasal movement (of *wh*-phrases) will then both become impossible. This prediction is correct, as we will now see. And as a result, it becomes possible to explain the salient properties of embedded verb-second clauses in Germanic.

4.3.1   Symmetric Verb-Second Languages

In the symmetric verb-second languages, the use of verb-second word order in embedded clauses follows a pattern that we should expect. In Yiddish and Icelandic—at least for some speakers and certain dialects—

the verb-second pattern appears to extend into embedded clause contexts quite freely, as illustrated in (69) and (70), taken from Vikner 1991 and Diesing 1990.

(69) *Icelandic*
    Jón efast   um að   á morgun fari María snemma á fætur.
    John doubts   that tomorrow will Mary get up   early

(70) *Yiddish*
    John tsveyfelt az   morgen   vet Miriam fri   oyfshteyn.
    John doubts   that tomorrow will Mary   early get-up

In both languages, embedded verb-second order is found in the complements to nonbridge verbs like nonassertive *doubt*. It is also possible to find verb-second order inside some relative clauses.[14]

(71) *Icelandic* (Rögnvaldsson 1984)
    a. Kennari sem slíkan þvætting ber á borð fyrir nemendur er til
       teacher   such nonsense tells to   his   students is to
       alls   vís.
       everything ready
       'A teacher who tells such nonsense to his students can do anything.'
    b. Flokkur sem um fjögurra ára   skeið hefur verið í stjórn
       party   for four   years ruler has   been in government
       tapaði kosningunum.
       lost   election
       'A party that for four years has been in the government lost the election.'

(72) *Yiddish*
    Der yid vos shabes   bay nakht vet Khayim zen.
    the man that Saturday at   night will Chaim see

The structures for such examples are clear and are to be expected. Topicalization in embedded clauses behaves like root topicalization, and involves a prior provocation of the topic by Fin before Top provokes it from [Spec, Fin]. So (69) is as shown in (73), and (71a) is structured as (74).

(73) Jón efast um [FcP að [TopP á morgun Top [FinP *t* fari-Fin [TP María *e* snemma á fætur *t*]]]].

(74) Kennari [FcP OP sem [TopP slíkan þvætting Top [FinP *t* ber-Fin [TP *t e* *t* á borð fyrir nemendur]]]] er til alls vís.

In general then, in the symmetric verb-second languages, structure (75) will always be permissible.

(75)

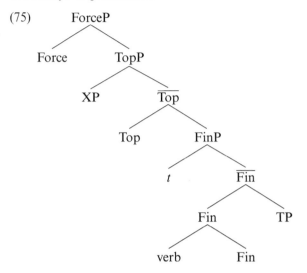

Since Force co-ocurs with TopP and FocP in these two languages, extraction from within a verb-second clause is expected to be possible. This seems true for at least some speakers of Icelandic and Yiddish. The data on this point has controversial status, but I will assume the most permissive interpretations of the data are accurate.[15]

(76) a. *Icelandic* (Rögnvaldsson 1984)
Þessar bækur hélt   ég að þér myndi ekki nokkur madur
these books thought I   that you would not any   man
lána.
lend
'These books, I thought that you would not lend to anyone.'
   b. *Yiddish* (Diesing 1990)
Vemen hot er nit gevolt az   ot di bikher zoln   mir gebn?
whom has he not wanted that the books should we give
'To whom did he not want us to give the books?'

The transparency of such clauses simply reflects the fact that nothing in these structures prevents Force from taking on a P-feature to attract a *wh*-phrase to its edge.

Unlike relative clauses, indirect questions in Icelandic and Yiddish resist combination with topicalization and verb-second word order. Schwartz and Vikner (1996) provide the data in (77) and (78).

(77) a. *Yiddish* (Diesing 1990)
       *Ikh veys nit ven   in tsimer iz di ku geshtanen.
       I   know not when in room is the cow stood
       'I don't know when the cow has stood in the room.'
    b. *Ikh veys nit vu   nekhtn   iz di ku geshtanen.
       I   know not where yesterday is the cow stood
       'I don't know where the cow stood yesterday.'
    c. Ikh veys nit far vos in tsimer iz di ku geshtanen.
       I   know not for what in room is the cow stood
       'I don't know why the cow is standing in the room.'

(78) a. *Icelandic*
       *Ég veit ekki af hvenær í herberginu hefur kýrin   staðið.
       I   know not   when   in room-the has   cow-the stood
       'I don't know when the cow has stood in the room.'
    b. *Ég veit ekki hvar í gær   hefur kýrin   staðið.
       I   know not where yesterday has   cow-the stood
       'I don't know where the cow stood yesterday.'
    c. *Icelandic*
       *Ég veit ekki af hverju í herberginu hefur kýrin   staðið.
       I   know not why   in room-the has   cow-the stood
       'I don't know why the cow has stood in the room.'

These sentences all contain embedded questions in which a topic, *in tsimer*/*í herberginu* or *nekhtn*/*í gær*, is fronted, presumably to the [Spec, Top] position. With the exception of (77c), all are ungrammatical.

The exceptionality of (77c) is probably to be attributed to the often peculiar behavior of *why* *wh*-phrases crosslinguistically. Schwartz and Vikner hypothesize that Yiddish *far vos* is merged directly into its surface position, much like Italian *perché* (Rizzi 1996), and I will make a similar claim. Then the pattern that emerges from (77) and (78) is that *wh*-movement from within TP is incompatible with topicalization in Icelandic and Yiddish, as it is in the asymmetric verb-second languages.

Since the more liberal range of topicalization in Icelandic and Yiddish reflects the lack of provocative [FORCE] features in Force, we should now conclude that this property of Force is simply different in *wh*-questions. In *wh*-questions, Yiddish and Icelandic behave like the asymmetric Germanic languages. In other words, Force may trigger *wh*-movement only when it bears provocative [uFORCE], with interpretable [FORCE] originating in Fin. Consider example (77a), with the embedded clause structure (79).

(79) ... [FcP ven Fc⁺ [TopP in tsimer Top [FinP *t* iz-Fin [TP di ku *t t*
geshtanen *e*]]]]

With the presence of TopP blocking head movement, Force cannot successfully provoke Fin, and the derivation crashes. And the same will be
true for the remaining ungrammatical examples in (77) and (78).

4.3.2 Asymmetric Verb-Second Languages

In embedded clauses, verb-second word order is severely constrained in
the asymmetric Germanic languages. In Dutch, for example, except for
in the asymmetric coordination structures already discussed, verb-second
word order in complement clauses is found only in the complement to
bridge verbs, a pattern typical of most of the other languages as well.[16]

In the earlier discussion of complementizer agreement (section 4.1) in
languages like Dutch, I concluded that embedded verb-second clauses
and "ordinary" embedded declaratives differ in whether Force provokes
Fin, producing structures like (80).

(80) a. *Embedded non-verb-second declarative*
... [FcP Fin-Force [FinP DP *e* [TP *t* T ...]]]
  b. *Embedded verb-second declarative*
... [FcP Force* ... [FinP XP T-Fin [TP *t e* ...]]]

In (80a), the provocative [FORCE] feature compels Fin to raise to adjoin to
Force; in (80b), this clearly does not occur. I will use the label Force*
(with the asterisk) to signify the complementizers that appear in embedded verb-second clauses and that do not attract Fin. Languages like
Dutch and Swedish then include both Force and Force* in their inventory of complementizer types.

In fact, there is clear evidence in Swedish that the Force* complementizer found with embedded verb-second clauses is distinct from those of
other declarative complementizers, despite their phonetic identity (Anders
Holmberg, personal communication). First, the *att* complementizer that
appears in verb-second constructions does not behave like the *att* we find
with other types of embedded declaratives. When not associated with a
verb-second clause, *att* may be omitted in complement clauses. But omis-
sion of *att* with verb-second clauses is impossible (Holmberg 1986). (The
verb-second status of the embedded clause in (81) can be seen from
the relative order of negative *inte* and the finite verb *köpte*.)

(81) *Per sa   han köpte   inte boken.
    Per said he   bought not book-the

The second difference between the *att* used in verb-second complements and the default *att* is found in conjoined complement clauses, where it is peculiarly constrained. When two such clauses are conjoined, the *att* complementizer appears *only* before the first clause. (Thanks to Anders Holmberg for the data.)

(82) *Swedish*
Jag tror   att Per äter inte kött och (*att) Anna dricker inte öl.
I   believe that Per eats not meat and that   Anna drinks not ale

This suggests that linear order plays some role in the acceptability of *att* in embedded verb-second clauses, which in turn leads me to suspect that something is involved outside the range of narrow syntax.

One way to unify the data in (81) and (82) would be by connecting it with the question of why the putative Force* complementizer is otherwise identical to the normal *att* complementizer. Recall that *dat*, the Dutch equivalent to *att*, seems to originate in the Fin position, and then raise to Force in non-verb-second contexts. In a verb-second clause, where Fin cannot raise to Force, *dat* obviously cannot find its way to the Force position in the same way. Instead, there must be a process that attaches *dat* directly to Force*. Let us refer to this process as *dat*-support, by analogy with the English *do*-support operation (Chomsky 1957). Like *do*-support, we may take *dat*-support to be a Spell-Out operation that provides morphological content to a head that requires it but cannot obtain it in the narrow syntactic derivation. Force* then lacks all phonetic content prior to *dat*-support. The same process can be assumed to occur in the other asymmetric languages in which an overt complementizer accompanies a verb-second word order. Swedish, for example, will require an equivalent operation of *att*-support. (In Swedish, too, *att* must then originate in the Fin position in non-verb-second clauses.)

The narrow syntactic structure of (82) will then be (83).

(83) Jag tror [$_{FcP}$ ∅ [$_{FinP}$ Per äter [$_{TP}$ inte kött]]]
                 och
        [$_{FcP}$ ∅ [$_{FinP}$ Anna   dricker [$_{TP}$ inte öl]]]

Suppose that Swedish *att*-support takes place with an empty Force* that is adjacent to a higher verb. In the narrow syntax, both Force* heads are presumably in equivalently high positions. Spell-Out linearizes this structure, though, and the result of linearization is that only the first empty Force* head is in a position for *att*-support to take place.

In contrast, in a nonconjoined embedded verb-second complement like (81), the empty Force* will always be in the right position for *att*-support, so the ungrammaticality of this sentence follows.

Modeling verb-second syntax includes coming to an understanding of the limited distribution of embedded verb-second clauses. If the structures in (80) are accurate, then this task will largely consist of a characterization of the conditions under which Force* is permitted.[17] From what is known of the problem, it is clear that several factors will be relevant, including the external context in which Force*P finds itself and the internal structure of Force*P. The latter is a good place to start.

Consider the Dutch example (84).

(84) Piet zei   dat dat boek kende hij niet.
    Pete said that that book knows he not

Here *dat boek* has been topicalized in the complement clause, which suggests the structure (85).

(85) ... [$_{Force*P}$ dat [$_{TopP}$ dat boek Top [$_{FinP}$ *t* kende-Fin [$_{TP}$ hij *t* niet *e*]]]]

The derivation of TopP in (85) will proceed in the same way as it does in root clauses: Fin takes on the [$\overline{MD}$] feature to attract the topic, and the ϕ-features of Fin then provoke T. Top then attracts the topic from [Spec, Fin] to [Spec, Top].

The first question raised by this structure is why the normal Force complementizer cannot be merged with TopP, in place of the Force* complementizer. An answer is forthcoming if we are careful about how provocation applies in this structure. Recall that the size of the copy of a phrase is determined in part by its location. When the goal of a P-feature is in the complement, then only the head of the complement phrase can be copied, and head movement results. Otherwise, a larger phrase is copied.

In (85), FinP is the complement to Top, and not to Force* (or Force), so Fin cannot raise to Force. If Force were used instead, it would provoke FinP instead of Fin, and the resulting structure would be (86).

(86) ... [$_{Force*P}$ [$_{FinP}$ *t* kende-Fin [$_{TP}$ hij *t* niet *e*]] dat [$_{TopP}$ dat boek Top *t*]]

But this structure is ill-formed in several ways. The topic *dat boek* does not c-command the clause that it is supposed to have scope over, which is probably semantically anomalous. And the force marker *dat* no longer introduces its clause[18] but is stuck in the middle, so it cannot be interpreted as a force marker.[19] It follows that Force can never take a TopP complement. Force*, however, does not provoke Fin or FinP, so it is allowed to co-occur with TopP.

The same considerations will apply even to subject-initial embedded verb-second clauses, as long as the subject is interpreted as the embedded clause topic. For example, in (87), the complementizer must again be Force* to escape the problems that arise if Fin(P) is provoked.

(87)   *Dutch*
       Piet zei [Force*P dat [TopP Hans Top [FinP *t* heeft-Fin [TP *t* dit boek
       Piet said   that   Hans   has   this book
       gelezen *e*]]].
       read

The external context in which Force*P is permitted is tricky to pin down precisely, because there tends to be a great deal of fluidity in speaker judgments on this point. But it seems more or less accurate to say that Force*P is permitted as the complement to bridge verbs, and barred elsewhere. This is true of Dutch, Frisian, mainland Scandinavian, German, and elsewhere. (Icelandic, Yiddish, and English are different and will be considered below.)

Why this environment permits Force*P complements is also tricky, but the fact that it involves a specific class of verbs and their complements indicates that this is in part a syntactic matter, which involves some sort of dependency between the verb and the Force* complementizer. In fact, this dependency resembles Baker's (1988) notion of *abstract incorporation* in important respects. Abstract incorporation, Baker says, has the same effect on the checking ability of the "incorporee" as overt incorporation does, which is to say it eliminates it. For example, the overt verb incorporation in (88a) is mirrored by the abstract verb incorporation in (88b). And in both, the effect of incorporation is to remove the ability of the lower verb to check accusative Case on its object. It is the matrix causative morpheme in both Chichewa and French that checks dative and accusative case on the arguments of the lower clause (Bobaljik and Branigan 2006).

(88) a. *Chichewa* (Baker 1988)
         Anyani   a-na-**meny**-ets-a   ana   kwa buluzi.
         baboons SP-PAST-hit-CAUS-ASP children to   lizard
         'The baboons made the lizard hit the children.'

b. *French*

Les babounes ont fait **frapper** les enfants au   lizard.
the baboons made   hit   the children to-the lizard
'The baboons made the lizard hit the children.'

If matrix bridge verbs incorporate Force* (abstractly), then we should expect that Force* will lack the checking properties that its unincorporated counterpart Force exhibits. The fact that Force* does not provoke Fin then follows automatically.

Other works have proposed that Force (=C) is incorporated overtly in other constructions (Pesetsky 1992; Bošković and Lasnik 2003). If abstract incorporation exists at all, we should not then be surprised to find it alongside its overt counterpart.

The abstract incorporation analysis of Force* also accounts for the fact that embedded verb-second clauses are islands in languages like Dutch, as the contrast in (89) illustrates.

(89) *Dutch* (Zwart 1997)

   a. Welke film zei je   dat Jan al   gezien had?
       which film said you that Jan already seen   had
       'Which film did you say that Jan saw already?'
   b. *Welke film zei je   dat Jan had al   gezien?
       which film said you that Jan had already seen

Consider how the *wh*-phrase in (89a) is extracted. Since ForceP is a phase, *welke film* must exit the downstairs clause via its [Spec, Force] edge. In other words, *dat* must take on a P-feature that attracts the *wh*-phrase. From [Spec, Force], the *wh*-phrase is accessible to further provocation from within the matrix clause.

In (89b), the same Phase Impenetrability Condition problem must be resolved for *wh*-movement to occur. But *dat* in this sentence is incorporated Force*, and therefore has no ability to take on a P-feature. Incorporated elements are inert with respect to checking of any kind. So the *wh*-phrase cannot be attracted to [Spec, Force] and long *wh*-movement from within the verb-second complement will always violate the Phase Impenetrability Condition.

In Schwartz and Vikner 1989, the islandhood of embedded verb-second complements is attributed to the presence of a topic phrase in the "escape hatch" position—that is, [Spec, C]. Zwart (1993) has critiqued this analysis on the grounds that it treats verb-second islands and *wh*-islands alike, while speakers do not assign the same judgments to the two types of island violations. In example (90), movement of *met welk mes* out of a

wh-island is relatively acceptable. Extraction from a verb-second complement is never this good.

(90) *Dutch* (Koster 1987)

    ?Met welk mes weet je niet hoe je dit brood zou kunnen
    with which knife know you not how you this bread   could
    snijden?
    cut
    'Which knife don't you know how you could cut this bread with?'

Zwart's objection, which I take to be valid (contra Branigan (1996b)),
does not apply to the present account, since verb-second islands and *wh*-
islands occur due to different principles of grammar. A *wh*-island occurs
when a *wh*-phrase in [Spec, Force] prevents another from escaping the
ForceP phase. A verb-second island arises from the complete inability of
Force* to attract anything from within its complement. The lesser degree
of unacceptability in *wh*-islands may reflect the near-success of an option
that is not available in verb-second islands. Suppose that Force in embedded questions has the ability to attract multiple *wh*-phrases, or at least
that this is not forbidden too strongly. Then a sentence like (90) might involve an earlier stage in the derivation in which the embedded ForceP
includes multiple *wh*-phrase specifiers:

(91) [$_{FcP}$ [$_{AdvP}$ hoe] [$_{PP}$ met welk mes] [$_{FinP}$ je *t t* dit brood zou kunnen
    snijden]].

In this structure, both *wh*-phrases are plausibly exempt from the Phase
Impenetrability Condition, since both are found at the edge of the ForceP
phase. The fact that the sentence does not become fully acceptable with
movement of the second specifier may then be a superiority effect, where
the second *wh*-phrase is not accessible because the first one is closer to the
attracting probe (Richards 1997). What Zwart's observation concerning
differences in grammaticality judgments shows us then is that pure Phase
Impenetrability Condition violations are rejected more strongly than
superiority violations with multiple specifiers in ForceP.

Other peculiarities of Force* support the Force*-incorporation hypothesis. DeHaan and Weerman (1986) and Zwart (1997) observe that Frisian
and Dutch enclitic subject pronouns are not allowed in embedded verb-
second clauses in those two languages respectively.

(92) a. *Frisian*

       Pyt sei dat hy/*er hie my sjoen.
       Pete said that he/scL had me seen
       'Pete said that he saw me.'

b. *Dutch*

Jan zei dat hij/*ie kende dat boek niet.

Jan said that he/SCL knew that book not

'Jan said that he didn't know that book.'

Zwart points out that proclitic subjects are permitted in the same context, though.

(93) *Dutch*

Jan zei dat je   leeft maar één keer.

Jan said that you-SCL live but   one time

'Jan said that you only live once.'

The difference is the element to which the clitic subject attaches itself. Clitics cannot attach to Force*, but they can attach to a following second-position verb. It is reasonable to suppose that the status of Force as an incorporated element is what interferes with the cliticization.

In German embedded verb-second clauses, no overt complementizer is present. Since the other Germanic languages examined have abstract incorporation of Force*, the natural conclusion is that German makes use of *overt* incorporation of the same element. Thus, the structure of a sentence like (94) will be (95).

(94) *German*

Anna glaubt, Hans-Peter habe das Buch gelesen.

Anna believes Hans-Peter has   the book read

(95) Anna [$_{vP}$ glaubt-Fc* [$_{Fc*P}$ *e* [$_{TopP}$ Hans-Peter Top [$_{FinP}$ *t* habe-Fin [$_{TP}$ *t* das Buch gelesen *e*]]]]]

Just as with the abstract incorporation structures, Force* will not check [FORCE] features or permit addition of a P-feature to attract a *wh*-phrase through [Spec, Force]. So verb-second word order results, and German embedded verb-second clauses, too, are extraction islands.[20]

(96) *German* (Schwartz and Vikner 1996)

a. Womit   glaubte sie hatte das Kind dieses Brot gegessen?

   what-with thought she had   the child this   bread eaten

   'What did she think the child had eaten this bread with?'

b. *Womit   glaubte sie das Kind hatte dieses Brot gegessen?

   what-with thought she the child had this   bread eaten

This difference between German and the other Germanic languages may be related to the use of "conjunctive" mood (Den Besten 1983) in German embedded verb-second clauses; the presence of conjunctive morphology on the verb signals clausal subordination, which makes the use of an overt complementizer superfluous.

Although Yiddish Force never provokes Fin, it still appears to be susceptible to overt incorporation, like its German counterpart. Incorporated Force* is silent in Yiddish, too. And like the other incorporated Force* heads, the Yiddish incorporated Force* forms an extraction island, as seen in (97).

(97) *Yiddish* (Diesing 1990)
    a.   Ven hostu   gezogt az   Max hot geleyent dos bukh?
        when have-you said   that Max has read   the book
        'When did you say that Max read the book?'
    b. *Ven hostu   gezogt Max hot geleyent dos bukh?
        when have-you said   Max has read   the book
    c.   Vos hot er nit gevolt as   mir zoln   leyenen?
        what has he not wanted that we should read
        'What did he not want us to read?'
    d. *Vos hot er nit gevolt mir zoln   leyenen?
        what has he not wanted we should read

As with the parallel verb-second islands in other languages, this follows from the inability of an incorporated Force* head to attract anything to the [Spec, Force] escape hatch position.

4.3.3 Embedded Verb-Second in English

Although English is asymmetric for the most part, it also patterns with Icelandic and Yiddish to a limited extent. For some English speakers, negative inversion is possible both in complement clauses and in other embedded contexts, although the interpretation of such structures will often be awkward. Speakers tend not to accept negative inversion in indirect questions, though.

(98) a.   Jane realized that never before had Sheila pitched a tent.
     b.   That on few earlier occasions had Ted mixed a martini would
        prove unfortunate.
     c.   It was with Mary at the helm that at no time was I concerned
        about my safety, not with John there.
     d. *Peter asked to whom at no point had Pierre offered his services.

For other speakers of English, the verb-second order inside a cleft structure or a relative clause is unacceptable, although sentences like (98a) and (98b) are fine.

There is only one way to account for this variation in the present model. Some speakers do allow *that* to originate in the Force position, although they do so only in a highly stylized speech register. When this occurs, English effectively becomes a symmetric language, in which Force does not attract Fin. As such, verb-second word order is possible, with Fin provoking a negative phrase that subsequently raises to [Spec, Top]. But just as Icelandic and Yiddish become asymmetric within indirect questions, English cannot switch to the symmetric pattern in the same context.

With noninverting topicalizations, English never seems to take on a fully symmetric character, although it is not entirely asymmetric here either. Topicalization in embedded clauses shares with embedded negative inversion the pattern of Force that does not provoke Fin. Thus in (99), where Top provokes *Mary* in its original TP-internal position, Force cannot provoke Fin because of the intervening presence of Top.

(99) I think that Mary, Bill told the news to *t* first.

The complementizer *that* in (99) must be a sort of dummy element, comparable to the Swedish *att* or Dutch *dat* that accompanies embedded verb-second structures. And like these others, the English dummy *that* cannot attract a *wh*-phrase. This can be seen in the island effect associated with normal topicalization, as evident from Lasnik and Saito's (1992) example (100).

(100) ??Which problem$_j$ do you think that Mary$_i$, Bill told t_i that John solved t_j?

The existence of this type of island follows directly from the interaction between Fin-provocation and *wh*-movement.

However, this raises a further question. Consider the two structures in (101).

(101) a. I told them [$_{FcP}$ that [$_{FocP}$ no finer tent Foc [$_{FinP}$ *t* had [$_{TP}$ Rosanna *e* pitched *t*]]]].
   b. *I asked them [$_{FcP}$ which tent Fc [$_{FinP}$ *t* had [$_{TP}$ Rosanna *e* pitched *t*]]].

In (101a), the negative focus *no finer tent* has to raise *via* [Spec, Fin], which in turn compels Fin to provoke T. But a similar derivational path is followed in (101b), where the *wh*-phrase *which tent* raises [Spec, Force] *via* [Spec, Fin], and yet the result is ungrammatical in standard English. And comparable structures are impossible in the other Germanic languages.

I will defer the analysis of this type of ungrammaticality to chapter 5.

Island effects that are ultimately comparable to those induced by embedded verb-second word order are found with embedded locative inversion structures as well. Rizzi and Shlonsky (2006) note the ungrammaticality of (102), for example.

(102) *When did he say that into the room walked Jack?

Like extraction from within a verb-second complement, movement of *when* in (102) is blocked by the usage of *that* as an inert force marker, which attracts neither Fin nor a specifier.

The reason *that* must be inert in this context involves slightly different factors than those involved in embedded verb-second complements. Although locative inversion clearly involves movement of the locative PP to the subject position, it also seems to require a second movement of the PP to a higher Ā-position (Stowell 1981; Dikken and Næss 1993; Rizzi and Shlonsky 2006). And this second movement takes place only with an appropriate landing site, which I take to be [Spec, Top], following Rizzi and Shlonsky.[21]

And like Rizzi and Shlonsky, I interpret the necessity of a second movement of the locative "subject" to reflect the fact that somehow the use of a PP in place of a normal nominal subject is more costly, so that it must be justified by making a later movement less costly. In other words, PPs can be attracted to subject positions only in order to get closer to a higher provocative head that will attract them later on. In this respect, locative inversion is driven by the same forces as verb-second word order, which exploits the [Spec, Fin] position to get a phrase closer to its ultimate landing site. But the mechanics are clearly different, since locative inversion is actually incompatible with verb-second word order.

I hypothesize for this case that T may take on the ability to provoke a locative goal, possibly with an areal ϕ-feature, and yet continue to agree with a normal nominal goal, but only when the locative goal also bears unvalued [uTOPIC] features. The locative PP will then raise to [Spec, T], where it will serve automatically as the goal for provocative Fin.[22] And the addition of a Top head to the structure will then ensure that the PP undergoes a final movement to [Spec, Top].

The consequence is that the structure of the complement clause for embedded locative inversion will be as in (103).

(103) He said [$_{\text{FcP}}$ that [$_{\text{TopP}}$ into the room Top [$_{\text{FinP}}$ t Fin [$_{\text{TP}}$ t walked Jack]]]].

As in the pure topicalization structure (100), the *that* complementizer cannot attract Fin in (103), since its complement is TopP rather than FinP. Again, this complementizer functions like the dummy elements that introduce embedded verb-second clauses in Dutch or Swedish, and for that reason it cannot attract a *wh*-phrase to [Spec, Force].

4.3.4 Embedded Inverted Interrogatives

Uniquely among the Germanic languages, some English dialects permit inverted word order in embedded questions such as (104).

(104) a. Gabrielle asked me could she go to the movie.
     b. I wonder where did the dog chase the cat.

In the most detailed study of this phenomenon to date, McCloskey (2007) elucidates the conditions under which this possibility is allowed. Two of his findings are especially significant in the present discussion. First, he shows that inverted embedded questions are permitted only in the complement to question-selecting verbs like *ask* and *wonder*, and marginally, if the matrix clause is negative or interrogative.

(105) (McCloskey 2007, 18)
     *I remember who did they hire.

(106) a. ?Do you remember who did they hire?
     b. ?I don't remember who did they hire.

Second, McCloskey demonstrates that in the same context, it is possible to prepose clause-internal adverbials past a complementizer or *wh*-phrase, which is otherwise unacceptable. Thus in (107a), the *after* phrase cannot be construed in the complement clause; (107a) cannot be synonymous with (107b).

(107) a. Peter decided after he fixed the truck that he would take a trip.
     b. Peter decided that after he fixed the truck he would take a trip.

But when the matrix verb is *ask* or *wonder*, the downstairs construal is marginally possible.

(108) a. ?Peter asked after he fixed the truck could we take a trip.
     b. ?Sheila was wondering when she finishes work where should she meet us.
     c. ?I wonder when you get home if we should order pizza.

As McCloskey observes, the word order in sentences like (108) immediately precludes an analysis in which the *wh*-phrase or polarity complementizer sits at the edge of the complement clause (i.e., in ForceP). If the preposed adverbials are in [Spec, Top], for example, *could*, *where*, and *if* must fit in somewhere lower down. It seems clear that FinP should be taken as the location for the markers of interrogativity in these examples, so that the structure in (108a) will include (109).

(109)

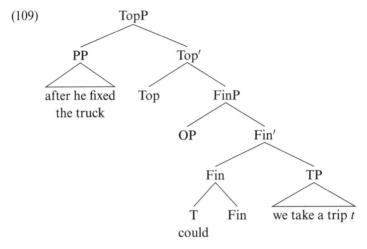

Similarly, examples (108b) and (108c) will have the structures in (110).

(110) a. Sheila was wondering [TopP when she finishes work [FinP where should-Fin [TP she *e* meet us *t t*]]].
      b. I wonder [TopP when you get home [FinP if [TP we should order pizza *t*]]].

This type of sentence is thus an example of normal topicalization of adverbial material accompanied by unusual use of FinP to host the interrogative marker in an embedded context. And the question that then arises is why Force does not attract the interrogative force marker in this case, and why the *if* complementizer originates in Fin instead of Force.

McCloskey himself draws slightly different conclusions from this data. His starting assumption is that auxiliary inversion is always movement of T to C, so that the fronted adverbials in sentences like (108) are external to CP and actually adjoined to CP. This approach, combined with the supposition that adjunction to arguments is not allowed, leads him to suppose a CP-recursion structure, in which an additional, silent C is present above the adverbial phrase that buffers the adjunction structure from the effects of the matrix verb. So McCloskey's analysis of (108a) would involve the structure (111).

(111)

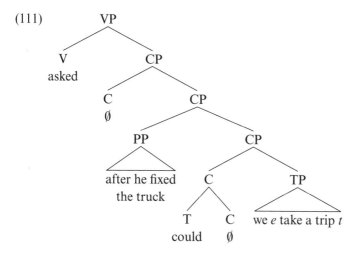

Nomenclature aside, McCloskey's analysis is very similar to the analysis I will offer. Adjunction to CP is much like movement to [Spec, Top], and the labels for the various flavors of "CP" are obviously provisional and of little significance. The key difference involves the presence of the silent upper complementizer in (111). McCloskey's argument for this head is based on the observation that adverbials cannot be adjoined to argumental CP, although they appear to be freely adjoined to root CP, as in (113).

(112) *I hope after supper that we can go for a walk.

(113) After supper where do you want to go?

It follows then that there must be a difference between the position of the embedded clause in (112) and those in (108), which is ensured by supposing a silent complementizer in the latter.

But the contrast between (112) and (113) is already derived from independently motivated principles in the present model. Since the *wh*-phrase in (113) does not raise all the way to Force (=C), the adverbial simply occupies [Spec, Top], just as it does in the comparable (114) examples.

(114) a. After supper we should take a walk.
       b. I hope that after supper we can take a walk.

There is then little reason to suppose that adjunction to any CP—root or embedded—is ever possible, and no further explanation is needed for the ungrammaticality of (112).

McCloskey himself notes the problematic status of the contrast in other
Germanic languages between root declaratives and interrogatives, where
the former disallow adverbial "adjunction" while the latter do not.

(115) a. *German* (Schwartz and Vikner 1996)
         *Gestern   Peter hat tatsächlich dieses Buch gelesen.
         yesterday Peter has actually   this   book read
         'Yesterday Peter actually read this book.'
      b. *Swedish*
         *Trots   allt Johan vill inte läsa de   här bökerna.
         despite all John will not read these here books
         'In spite of everything, John will not read these books.'

(116) a. *German*
         Wenn wir nach Hause kommen, was   sollen wir kochen?
         when we to   house come   what should we cook
         'When we get home, what should we cook?'
      b. *Swedish* (Wechsler 1991)
         I en stad   som Fremont vem skulle inte vara uttråkad?
         in a   town like Fremont who would not be   bored
         'In a town like Fremont, who wouldn't be bored?'

If adjunction to CP were allowed in root clauses, then the preposed
adverbials should be acceptable in the (115) sentences. This contrast is,
of course, expected in the provocation model, where the adverbials in
both cases are raised to [Spec, Top]. In the ungrammatical (115) examples, the problem is not in the position occupied by the adverbials but
rather in the derivational path that places them there. Because the [Spec,
Fin] position could have been made use of by the adverbial en route to
[Spec, Top], Fin should have provoked the finite verb in T to produce a
normal verb-second topicalization structure. In the (more) grammatical
(116) sentences, [Spec, Fin] can only host the *wh*-phrases—which have
nowhere else to go—so it is not free for the preposed adverbial. Top
therefore provokes the adverbial topics directly in their TP-internal original position, just as it does in the English examples (113) and (114a).

McCloskey's argument for a higher null C appears to lack force, and I
conclude that the proper structure for English indirect questions with
inverted word order is that in (109). The dialects in which this is possible
allow a complement clause that lacks a Force head for verbs like *ask* and
wonder. Question formation internal to the complement clause must then
follow the pattern for root clauses, by taking advantage of the [Spec, Fin]
Ā-position to allow *wh*-movement.

As for the special properties of the question-selecting matrix predicates, I have nothing to suggest beyond what McCloskey proposes. His claim, following Groenendijk and Stokhof 1984 and much subsequent work, is that verbs like *ask* take complements of a different semantic type than verbs like *remember* do. Evidently, the semantic type for *remember* complements requires the presence of a Force head in phrase structure, while the semantic type for *ask* complements does not.

4.3.5 Force and Long Topicalization

Chomsky (1977) showed that unbounded topicalization is subject to the same constraints as *wh*-movement, and concluded that the two represent the same operation. What this implies for a sentence like (117a) is that it should involve the same movement strategy for extraction from the complement clause as (117b) does.

(117) a. Those letters, I wish that Bart had never promised he would send.
      b. Which letters do you wish that Bart had never promised he would send?

In both cases, evidence from *wh*-islands shows that extraction out of the complement clauses must make use of the [Spec, Force] escape hatch. Assuming the Phase Impenetrability Condition, this is necessary on theory-internal grounds anyway. In the *wh*-movement case, movement to [Spec, Force] is driven by an [*u*FORCE] feature added to the Force head. The same should then be true in the long topicalization case.

It must be concluded that topics bear a [FORCE] feature, just like *wh*-phrases and complementizers. Unlike these others, topics seem not to be interpreted as force markers—the [FORCE] feature on a topic is simply a formal feature that allows certain ends to be met. In Pesetsky and Torrego's (2007) terminology, the [FORCE] feature in a topic is valued but is not interpretable. In that case, [FORCE] on topics must be deleted when it has fulfilled its formal role of driving movement.[23]

Since fronted topics bear a [FORCE] feature, we might simplify the inventory of features involved in Ā movement by identifying the hitherto mysterious [$\overline{\text{MD}}$] feature with [FORCE]. In that case, one of the main difference between English and the verb-second Germanic languages would be that [*u*FORCE] may be added to both Force and Fin in the non-English languages. English, of course, adds only [MD] to Fin. In this light, let us compare the course of long topicalization in German, Swedish, and English:

(118) a. *German* (Müller 1995)

  [$_{TopP}$ Hygrometer [$_{FinP}$ *t* glaube [$_{TP}$ ich [$_{FinP}$ *t* würde [$_{TP}$ Antje *t*
  hygrometers   believe   I   would   Antje
  mögen]]]]].
  like

  b. *Swedish*

  [$_{TopP}$ Lars [$_{FinP}$ *t* tror   [$_{TP}$ Ingrid [$_{FcP}$ *t* att   Karin inte
  Lars   believes   Ingrid   that Karin not
  älskar *t*]]]].
  loves

  c. [$_{TopP}$ Beans [$_{FinP}$ I don't believe [$_{FcP}$ *t* that anyone really likes
  t]]].

In the German (118a), derived with inversion in both root and embedded clauses, [*u*FORCE] is added to Fin in the embedded clause, and then again to Fin in the matrix clause. The last step of topicalization, in which *hygrometer* raises from [Spec, Fin] to [Spec, Top], involves the provocative [TOP] feature of Top, and not [FORCE]. In fact, the [FORCE] feature of *hygrometer* should be deleted when provocation is complete in the root clause, because the topic cannot be interpreted as a force marker. In the Swedish (118b), [*u*FORCE] is added to Force in the embedded clause and then to Fin in the matrix clause, and once again, the final stage involves attraction of *Lars* by Top from [Spec, Fin]. In the English (118c), [*u*FORCE] is added only to Force in the embedded clause, and the matrix clause Top has to attract the topic *beans* from within TP, and not from [Spec, Fin].

4.4 Conclusion

In the voluminous, detailed, and sophisticated body of literature on Germanic word order, there are a handful of basic approaches to the issues addressed here. The literature is largely uniform in assuming that *wh*-movement is a process of EPP-satisfaction, driven by a *wh*-checking procedure. The pervasive subject/nonsubject asymmetries found in questions and relative clauses have remained mysterious, and the recent minimalist literature has left this type of problem unresolved.

More dramatic disagreements in the literature emerge in the analysis of verb-second word order. In one school of thought, typified by the work of Travis (1984) and Zwart (1997), verb-second word order involves heterogeneous structures, with subject-initial clauses and topic-initial clauses treated as distinct. Anderson's (1993) asyntactic approach might be included in this type of theory as well. In this approach, root clause subjects typically remain in [Spec, T], while topics raise to a higher position. By maintaining a distinction between the two, analyses of this type have been able to cope with the fact that many subjects are simply not topics, and with many more subtle empirical differences between subject-initial and topic-initial verb-second clauses as well. (Zwart, in particular, has cataloged such differences exhaustively.) Explaining the position of the verb has required some technical gymnastics, though.

In the P-model developed here, the idea that subjects and topics show different behavior is preserved, but not by having them necessarily occupy different positions. Subjects and nonsubject topics are both attracted to [Spec, Fin] in this model, but the features that attract them are different. This distinction makes it possible to accommodate the significant results of the Zwart/Travis approach without accepting the claim that there is no single structural locus for verb-second word order.

The competitor approach in the literature has maintained that all verb-second word order (in a single language) involves the same structures. Thus, Den Besten (1983) claims that verb-second word order centers on the COMP position, a claim adopted in updated form by Vikner (1991) and Schwartz and Vikner (1989, 1996). Others have claimed that verb-second word order is situated in TP, whether for particular languages (Icelandic, in Thrainsson 1986; Yiddish, in Diesing 1990) or for all of non-English Germanic (Müller 1995). In general, this second approach has found it easier to provide accounts of the facts that embedded verb-second clauses are restricted in their distribution (in the asymmetric languages) and they are islands for extraction. The more liberal nature of Icelandic, and particularly of Yiddish, has proved problematic for those who locate verb-second word order in "COMP," while the limited island-hood of Icelandic embedded verb-second clauses is troublesome if these clauses are simply TPs.

In the P-model, the fact that all verb-second word order involves FinP makes it relatively easy to explain the position of the finite verb. The distinction between symmetric and asymmetric languages follows from properties of Fin and Force, rather than from wholly distinct structures used for topicalization. And these same properties—[uFORCE] features in Force, and complementizers in Fin—provide an automatic account of verb-second islands, and (with Force incorporation) of the restricted distribution of embedded verb-second word order in some languages.

In short, the model presented here achieves the major results of previous work into Ā movement and verb-second word order and avoids their pitfalls. And it provides an explanation for the very subtle distinctions between the symmetric Germanic languages (Icelandic and Yiddish) and the asymmetric ones, which have confounded other theories. I would maintain that this result offers strong support for the idea that the single syntactic process of provocation applies equally to heads and full phrases.

4.5 Appendix: Selection of Clausal Complements

The claim was put forth in chapter 4 that some embedded finite clauses are bare FinP and not full ForceP structures. Bare FinP appears in subject relatives, and in some dialects of English, as complements to specific interrogative-selecting predicates. But it is clear that bare FinP is not allowed in many other contexts. So the principles that control which types of clausal complements are allowed for which context become important for the present discussion. An understanding of these principles will become crucial in chapter 5, when I examine constraints on successive cyclic Ā movement.

First I will sketch out how the choice between ForceP and FinP is grammatically controlled in general. Then the focus will be an examination of specific cases, and the broader issue of how the "size" of embedded clauses is generally determined.

Two types of embedded finite clauses have been identified already. Normal declaratives, questions, and relative clauses are full ForceP structures, with FinP as the complement of Force, and TP, the complement of Fin. In some relative clauses and some indirect questions (in some dialects), no Force projection appears, so that FinP constitutes the entire embedded clause. A third type of finite clause seems to be unattested: bare TP, with neither Fin nor Force accompanying it. If finite TPs were acceptable in complement position, then reflexive/reciprocal expressions should be permissible in their subject position, as in

(119) *Jean and Clint imagine each other like trad jazz.

I have little new to say about the unacceptability of bare finite TP, and the literature already includes a large enough number of speculations on why such structures are not allowed. It may be that finite Tense needs somehow to be sheltered from the influence of Tense in the matrix clause (Gueron and Hoekstra 1988). And it is not implausible that some portions of the semantic content of Tense originate in Fin, and are assigned to Tense to be realized there (Chomsky 2007). Whatever the reason, the generalization seems clear enough: finite TP must be accompanied by Fin.

Once Fin is added to a clause, the properties of Fin itself ensure that a fairly complicated syntax must accompany it. At least in the asymmetric Germanic languages, finite Fin is the location where force-marking complementizers originate. Such complementizers are normally subject to interpretation only at the clause edge. This property of Fin is intrinsically at odds with the presence of provocative ϕ-features in the same position, because these P-features ensure a specifier for FinP, which bumps the complementizer from the clausal edge. A solution can be found for this conflict if Force is merged with FinP and if Force then attracts the complementizer to the new edge of the clause. It follows that Force will often be a required component of embedded clauses even if this head itself makes no substantial contribution to the meaning of the clause.

The implication is that Force must often be present in the structure even if it is not visible. Thus in (120), the complement to *forget* must be ForceP, as in (120a); the bare FinP posited in (120b) must be an illegitimate analysis for this case.

(120) a.   Jean forgot [$_{ForceP}$ (that) the window was open].
      b.   *Jean forgot [$_{FinP}$ the window Fin was open].

The impossibility of the structures in (120b) is not obvious from the surface strings, but can be easily verified. If bare FinP was a possible complement for verbs like *forget*, then we should not find the sort of null complementizer "licensing" effects noted by Bošković and Lasnik (2003), which are evident from the contrasts in (121) and (122).

(121) a.   *It seemed at that time [$_{FcP}$ [$_{Fc}$ ∅] David had left].
      b.   It seemed at that time [$_{FcP}$ that David had left].

(122) a.   *They suspected and we believed [$_{FcP}$ ∅ Peter would visit the hospital].
      b.   They suspected and we believed [$_{FcP}$ that Peter would visit the hospital].

Bošković and Lasnik propose that the null complementizer is licensed by a morphological merger operation that combines it with an adjacent verb to its left.[24] Fin, which is usually silent, does not need any contextual licensing, so the conditions that are not satisfied in (121a) and (122a) must apply to a null Force head, which must perforce be present. The conclusion has to be that finite complement clauses normally need to include Force, whether we see it or not.

A second solution to the problem that arises when a specifier keeps Fin from the edge of its clause would be to eliminate the specifier somehow. In a relative clause like (123), for example, it is the absence or silence of the relative pronoun that allows the complementizer in Fin to be interpreted.

(123) the wind [$_{FinP}$ that [$_{TP}$ blew down the tent]]

In principle, movement of the specifier to a position external to its clause should have the same effect. We might then expect that bare FinP complements should be found when the subject is extracted under Ā-movement. Phenomena like the French *que-qui* alternation (Kayne 1972) support this expectation.[25] In fact, the appearance of the *qui* complementizer in a declarative complement can be taken as a direct manifestation of a force-marking Fin that does not raise to Force.[26]

(124) Qui imagines-tu [$_{FinP}$ *t qui* [$_{TP}$ a   écrit   cet article]]?
        who think-you   has written this article
        'Who do you think wrote this article?'

Qui may appear only in case the subject is extracted, as can be seen from (125).

(125) *Ils   imaginent qui Marie a   rit.
         they think   that Marie has laughed

Subject extraction from a finite clause in French is actually impossible when a full ForceP complement appears. The ungrammaticality of (126) is because the *que* complementizer must be the realization of Fin adjoined to Force, so that *que* does not appear unless ForceP is present.

(126) *Qui imagines-tu *qu'*a   écrit   cet article?
         who think-you   has written this article

This is what the *that*-trace effect amounts to, at least in French: an inability to extract the specifier of FinP from inside a ForceP complement.[27] (I defer a more detailed examination of the *that*-trace effect until chapter 5.)

In English, subject extraction in declaratives is usually possible only when there is no *that* complementizer. It appears to be possible to extend the analysis of French *qui* to this situation.

(127) Which car does Bill insist *t* was parked in his space?

Such an extension is a trivial technical affair. In (127), for example, it is possible to maintain that the complement clause is a bare FinP, rather than a full CP. The head of the complement clause would then be a null token of Fin, a hypothesis that is tenable since Fin appears often to lack phonetic content in English. Like *qui*, the particular Fin in (127) does not raise to Force, but remains in situ. Like French *qui*, English Fin that appears in situ in a declarative complement can be interpreted as a force marker by virtue of the lack of a specifier at the left edge of the clause.

There is evidence that this is more than merely a technical analogy. Consider the data in (128).

(128) a. Penny feels (*sincerely) Paul should be given another chance.
    b. Penny feels sincerely that Paul should be given another chance.
    c. How many chances does Penny feel (*sincerely) Paul should be given?

As observed in Stowell 1981, in the normal case, a silent complementizer must be adjacent to a matrix verb. This descriptive generalization is consistent with Bošković and Lasnik's (2003) idea that null declarative C (=Force) must undergo Morphological Merger with the verb to its left. If the verb is not adjacent to C, then no Morphological Merger can take place. Notice that A-bar movement out of the complement clause in (128c) has no effect on the adjacency effect with null C.

But when the subject is extracted, the adjacency effect disappears, as in (129).

(129) Who does Penny feel sincerely should be given another chance?

We may conclude that there is a significant structural difference between subject extraction clauses like (129) and clauses with the normal null declarative complementizer. Suppose now that English subject extraction patterns with French subject extraction. Then the structure of (129) will be (130):[28]

(130) Who does Penny feel sincerely [$_{FinP}$ *t* Fin [$_{TP}$ *t* should be given another chance]]?

Bošković and Lasnik (2003) observe as well that Right Node Raising examples like (131) are impossible with null complementizers.

(131) a. They believed, and Mary claimed, *(that) John would murder Peter.
    b. Who did they believe, and Mary claim, *(that) John would murder?

This pattern again reflects the need of a null complementizer to undergo Morphological Merger with a matrix head, which is impossible if the null complementizer is deleted in the first conjunct.

With subject extraction in the complement clause, however, no overt complementizer is required (or allowed) in parallel Right Node Raising structures.

(132) Who did they believe, and Mary claim, would murder Peter?

Again, the ability of FinP to appear as a bare complement clause under the right conditions is what explains the acceptability of (132). Both *believe* and *claim* in (132) take a FinP complement, where Fin is a legitimate force marker since it is at the left edge of its clause. And the entire structure is legitimate because Fin is not subject to special licensing conditions that are disrupted by Right Node Raising, unlike null declarative C.

So it seems that English and French differ in only one, quite superficial respect with respect to the conditions under which subject Ā-movement will be possible. In both languages, Fin has no phonetic content when it heads the complement to an argumental C. In French, it takes the form *qui* when it appears in its base position. In (standard) English, Fin has no phonetic content even when it does not raise to incorporate into C.

For those English dialects that do permit subject extraction with an overt *that* complementizer (Sobin 1987), we may now simply assume that Fin may be realized as *that* when it is not the complement to a higher C. The dialectal variation then reduces to a difference in the phonetic form of a single functional head (Branigan 1996a).

Further evidence that subject extraction allows bare FinP complements to appear can be found by looking at some well-known exceptions to the general Case-marking patterns in infinitives. Ruwet (1972) observed the contrast in (133) and (134).

(133) *Louise sait   Pierre être   intelligent.
       Louise knows Pierre to-be intelligent

(134) Pierre, qui Louise sait   être   intelligent
       Pierre who Louise knows to-be intelligent

Unlike English, French does not permit bare infinitival TP complements to verbs of knowing. Like English finite TP, French TP seems to require a buffer to separate it from the matrix clause. Simple ECM is impossible in French, therefore, because the ForceP phase boundary precludes any Agree operation involving a matrix verb and the embedded subject. Bare infinitival FinP is possible, however, under the same circumstances as bare finite FinP. In other words, infinitival FinP is an acceptable complement to bridge verbs, as long as Fin appears at the edge of the clause. This is possible only when the subject is extracted, and the subject trace, deleted. The relevant structure of (134), then, is (135).

(135) Pierre, qui$_i$ Louise sait [$_{FinP}$ t_j Fin [$_{TP}$ t_i être intelligent]]

With no ForceP present in the complement clause, the verb *savoir* may Agree with the trace in [Spec, T], assigning Case in the process.

Similar observations have been made of English contrasts in (136) by Kayne (1984). With matrix predicates in the *wager*-class (Pesetsky 1992), simple ECM is impossible.

(136) a. *They assured me the permit to have been issued.
      b. What permit did they assure you to have been issued?

(137) a. *Karin wagered the election to be fixed.
      b. the election that Karin wagered to be fixed

Again, Ā-movement of the subject of an infinitival complement is necessary in order to allow Case assignment to take place. The treatment of the analogous French examples carries over to the English as well. Consider (136). We need only suppose that infinitival TP cannot appear as the second complement of *assure*, although bare FinP can, if only Fin appears at the clause edge. In (136a) the presence of the subject *the permit* in [Spec, Fin] keeps Fin from its clause edge, so the structure is illegitimate at the LF interface. But with extraction of the subject in (136b), Fin does appear at the edge. The matrix verb then is able to agree with the [Spec, T] trace and Case assignment takes place, as it must. Similarly in (137), *wager* does not accept a bare TP complement, so that it can assign Case to the subject only if subject extraction makes a nonphasal bare FinP complement acceptable.

Not all bare FinP complements appear to be constrained in the same way. With finite clauses, and with the infinitives just discussed, bare FinP is permitted only if Fin appears at the edge. Some *irrealis* infinitival complements are less constrained; infinitival complements to *want*-class predicates[29] may be FinP even with the subject remaining in [Spec, Fin]. Thus, in (138), the complement clause is a bare FinP.

(138) Jim wants [$_{FinP}$ his sister Fin [$_{TP}$ t to stop smoking]].

As FinP is nonphasal, *want* may assign Case directly to the subject trace in [Spec, T].

Chomsky and Lasnik (1977) and Chomsky (1981) analyzed sentences like (138) as equivalent to *for-to* infinitives, and supposed that Case is assigned to the subject by a silent version of the *for* complementizer, internal to the embedded clause. But as Pesetsky (1992) points out, the embedded subject is dependent on the matrix verb for Case in the same way in (138) as with simpler ECM complements. So passivization of the matrix verb prevents it from assigning Case in both (139a) and (139b).

(139) a. *It is wanted Karin to stop smoking.
       b. *It was believed Karin to have already stopped.

Since [Spec, Fin] is an Ā position, the subject cannot undergo A-movement, although Ā movement is allowed.

(140) a. *Karin is wanted to stop smoking.
       b.   Who does Jim want to stop smoking?

This contrast is due to the general prohibition on improper movement, which blocks movement from an Ā position to an A position.

Want-class predicates marginally allow full ForceP irrealis infinitival complements, too. With lexical subjects, such complements must include the *for* complementizer in Force.

(141) Jim hoped with all his heart [$_{\text{FcP}}$ for [$_{\text{FinP}}$ Karin Fin [$_{\text{TP}}$ *t* to stop smoking]]].

The structure of the complement clause in this case is clearly identical to that of other *for-to* infinitives: ForceP, with *for* in the Force position.

(142) [$_{\text{FcP}}$ for [$_{\text{FinP}}$ Karin Fin [$_{\text{TP}}$ *t* to quit smoking]]] would make Jim happy.

In all such *for-to* infinitives, it must be *for* that Case-marks the subject trace in [Spec, T]. Since FinP does not impose a phase boundary, there is no impediment to Case assignment in this structure.[30]

As with finite complements, subjects in [Spec, Fin] can be extracted from bare FinP complements, but not from full ForceP.[31]

(143) *Who does Jim want (desperately) [$_{\text{FcP}}$ for *t* to stop smoking]?

This so-called *for*-trace constraint is then simply another case of the same general rule that controls extraction from [Spec, Fin].

Clausal complements to English perception verbs and causatives behave similarly to irrealis infinitival complements.

(144) a. Beth heard the door open.
       b. We watched the clouds grow dark.
       c. This new data made us reevaluate our approach.

Like the complements to *want*-class verbs, the complements in (144) permit Ā-movement of the subject, but not A-movement.

(145) a. Which door did she hear open?
       b. *The door was heard open.
       c. Which clouds did you watch grow dark?
       d. *The clouds were watched grow dark.
       e. Who did this new data make reevaluate their approach?
       f. *We were made reevaluate our approach.

The complements in this case are not infinitival, given the absence of *to*. Instead, the verb form appears to be subjunctive, since it does not change its form to agree with the subject (Branigan 1992; Hale and Keyser 1993). In this respect, English patterns with modern Greek, which also selects subjunctive clausal complements for perception verbs. Unlike irrealis subjunctives in English, the subjunctive complements to perception verbs are not full ForceP clauses, but bare FinP instead. Example (144a) has the structure (146).

(146) Beth heard [$_{FinP}$ the door Fin [$_{TP}$ *t* T open]].

This is why the matrix verb has access to the subject trace and is able to assign accusative Case to it. But since [Spec, Fin] is an Ā position, A-movement of the subject remains impossible.

Hoekstra and Bennis (1989) observe a similar pattern in Swedish perception verb complements, with one additional interesting wrinkle.

(147) a. Jag hör Peter sjunga en sang.
         I   hear Peter sing a song
      b. *Peter blev hörd sjunga en sang.
         Peter was heard sing a song
      c. Peter hördes   sjunga en sang.
         Peter was-heard sing a song

Like English, Swedish appears to take bare FinP complements to perception verbs, so that the matrix verb can assign Case to the subject of the complement but A-movement of the subject is impossible. Unlike English, however, Swedish makes use of reflexive passives, as in (147c), and these are compatible with the FinP complements. If we assume that the reflexive form *hördes* is formed syntactically, by movement of the clitic suffix *-s* from [Spec, Fin] onto the matrix verb, then the derivation of (147c) seems unproblematic. This Swedish clitic movement from an Ā-position is quite similar to what occurs in French *faire* causatives, in fact, where clitic subjects raise from an Ā position at the left edge of the complement clause to the usual preverbal position in front of *faire* (Bobaljik and Branigan 2006).

(148) Paul *les*   fera   refaire [*t e* le   menage   ].
       Paul them make-FUT redo   the housework
       'Paul will make them redo the housework.'

5 Provoking Trace Deletion

5.1 Introduction

The central claim in the analyses I am proposing is that probe-driven movement is based on a complex operation that generates a distinct copy of a category containing the goal. It is precisely because the two copies formed are independent linguistic objects that the copy must merge with the original tree structure that contains its source. This appears to me to be the most significant difference between my analysis of movement and that of Chomsky (2004, 2007). If movement is driven by the needs of the target of movement—such as an EPP property—then there is no necessity that two separate phrases be involved. It is certainly coherent, and in some respects more elegant, to say that a single phrase occupies multiple positions in a phrase marker (see Chomsky 2008, 1995, among others, for discussion).

In section 2.5, one argument was presented to show that movement does involve the formation of distinct copies. This final chapter develops a second, more complex, argument to the same effect.

I will show that a substantial number of "constraints" that restrict movement in, through, and to the left periphery reduce to one general pattern that bars movement from [Spec, Fin] to [Spec, Force]. One special cases of this generalization is the *that*-trace effect. With this pattern established, I then show that it reflects a failure to delete intermediate Ā-traces in successive cyclic Ā-movement, and that this failure induces a crash at LF. And the reason such traces must be deleted can only be that they constitute linguistic objects distinct from the other copies in an interpretable, binary, operator-variable chain.

The structure of the argument to be presented is as follows. Under standard assumptions about the interpretation of quantificational structures like questions, focal statements, and so on, such structures must contain, minimally, two quantificational elements. One of them—the "trace"—is a restricted variable that occupies a clause-internal position, and this position is associated with its predicate-argument semantics. In other words, a variable is an argument if it is assigned a θ-role, and something else if not. The other necessary part of quantificational structures is some way to identify the type of quantification and the domain of quantification, to identify the scope. In common usage, this second element is called the operator.

If these assumptions are at all accurate, then any theory of Ā-movement must include some mechanism by which operator-variable structures may be provided to the LF interface. Otherwise no quantificational meanings would be possible.

There are two possible ways to ensure the right result. The syntactic derivation itself may produce operator-variable chains, thereby minimizing the work that needs to be done at the interface. The alternative is that the syntax proper provides structures that do not contain anything like operators or variables, but that carry enough information to allow a mapping procedure to construct operators and variables.

The provocation model falls into the first of these approaches. As discussed in section 2.5, chains formed by provocation are subject to internal reconstruction, depending on the type of provocative feature being valued. Take a standard embedded *wh*-question structure as in (1), for example.

(1) ... [$_{\text{FcP}}$ which tent Fc [the bike was traded for]]

In this case, interrogative Force provokes *which tent*, forming the chain (*which tent*^{1}, Force, *which tent*^{2}), with *which tent*^{1} external to the original ForceP. The valued [WH] feature is shared by the three members of this chain, but it is interpretable only in the two *wh*-phrases. What is more, the presence of Force in the chain identifies it as an Ā-chain, from which an operator-variable structure must be formed. Therefore, to make the chain interpretable as a whole, enough content is deleted from its members to produce the improved chain for LF: (WH x, [$_{\text{DP}}$ [$_{\text{D}}$ x] [$_{\text{N}}$ tent]]).

The second member of this chain contains the variable, so the deletion process already provides one of the two minimal components for the quantification. When the head of this chain is merged to become the specifier for ForceP, its position establishes the scope of the quantification, and the *wh*-content signifies the type of quantification required.

Chomsky's (2004) model seems to fall into the other camp, in which mapping at LF establishes the operator-variable structure from a less articulated syntactic input. For Chomsky, phrasal movement does not involve distinct categories, but only a single category occupying multiple positions. It is immediately clear that the syntactic derivation will not have the option of producing an operator-variable structure, because a single category cannot have two separate identities, with different content. This necessitates a quite different analysis of the interpretation of (1). The *wh*-phrase *which tent* will be presented *as is* to the LF interface, albeit in several different syntactic positions. The interpretation procedure at LF must then identify the scope of quantification by finding the highest position occupied by *which tent*. The type of quantification will come from the [*u*WH] feature, of course. And the variable will be understood in the topmost A-position occupied by this phrase.

An analogy may make clearer the differences that concern me between the two conceptions of phrasal movement. Chomsky's notion of a category occupying multiple positions in a phrase marker can be likened to a person within some large institution—a church, university, club, or corporation, for example—who plays several institutional roles simultaneously, such as secretary-treasurer, webmaster, and social director, or perhaps lecturer, director of such-and-such a lab, and dean. We can describe an individual of this type as "zealous"; a "zealot" is then someone who occupies multiple institutional positions. And "zealotry" would be the process of taking on extra positions.

Consider what happens when a zealot suffers a heart attack or some other ailment that prevents her from working. The effects are not confined to a single unit of the institution—the financial records get messed up, the web page becomes outdated, and there are no Christmas parties arranged, for example.

Continuing with the analogy, the notion of provocation can be likened to a cloning process. In a parallel institution, perhaps with a shortage of administrative talent but a very sophisticated biology department, suppose that the dean, in need of a department head and a director of the lab, has himself cloned twice so that his clones can take on these other jobs. There are no zealots in this scenario, because the result is that each individual occupies a single position. If later the dean gets hit by a truck, then the department head and lab director can continue to function.

Chomsky's (2004) position is that movement produces syntactic zealots. Phrasal movement is zealotry. The argument I develop in favor of provocation in this chapter goes like this: movement operations exhibit properties different from those we expect in zealotry. Specifically, characterizing Ā-movement seems to require that we recognize the presence of extra "individuals" who could not be present in a model with only zealots. And to the extent that the provocation model accounts for the extra individuals, it is supported over models in which no extra copies are required to characterize movement.

Viewed from another angle, my intention here is to bring out the relationship between the peculiar constraints on successive cyclic movement that apply to elements in the left periphery and the general architecture of the derivation. The phenomenon that will guide this discussion is the *that*-trace effect.

5.2 *That*-Trace Effects

5.2.1 Background
One reason for the prolonged attention paid in the literature to the *that*-trace effect must be that it is, on the face of it, a dysfunctional grammatical phenomenon, one that simply prevents us from saying certain sentences. It seems to follow its own logic, which has little to do with general locality constraints, economy considerations, or strategies to avoid ambiguity. And because the *that*-trace effect is so bizarrely dysfunctional, it is tempting to suppose that it exists as a reflection of something deep in the structure of Universal Grammar, which we have perhaps failed to notice so far.[1]

The classical *that*-trace effect is illustrated in (2):

(2) a.   What did Peter claim [*t* had happened]?
    b. *What did Peter claim that [*t* had happened]?

(3) a.   What did Peter claim that [Penny had fixed *t*]?
    b.   How did Peter claim that [Penny had fixed it *t*]?

What the contrast in (2) shows is that some principle of grammar blocks subject *wh*-movement past a local complementizer in English. In (3), though, we see that this principle does not constrain movement of nonsubjects, both arguments and adjuncts.

A large part of the difficulty in understanding *that*-trace effects stems from the problem that there does not seem to be a natural class of elements that are subject to it. The canonical examples of this effect look like (4), where the presence of the *that* complementizer interferes with *wh*-movement of the subject. Familiar poverty-of-the-stimulus arguments show that this pattern should arise from innate principles. But, as has already been observed at several earlier points, the same pattern is found sometimes with nonsubjects (in locative inversion). Analogous restrictions are found with subject extraction in nonfinite clauses. And depending on the language/dialect, the effect may not arise at all, or it may require a different form for the complementizer to allow subject extraction to take place.

(4) Which pen do you find (*that) writes the smoothest.

The analysis of clausal complements presented in the appendix to chapter 4 goes a long way in clarifying the context in which *that*-trace effects are found. Successful subject extraction is possible when the subject in [Spec, Fin] is removed from a bare FinP complement, and other categories that occupy [Spec, Fin] are subject to the same constraint. The presence of *that* in (4) signifies that ForceP is present in the complement clause—at least in those dialects where the *that*-trace effect is found. But the explanatory problem has not been addressed. ForceP does not generally interfere with successive cyclic Ā-movement. Why then should ForceP make it more difficult to extract something from [Spec, Fin]?

Two basic strategies can be pursued to explain why some particular set of elements is subject to any given grammatical constraint. One way is to relate the constraint directly to the set. The other way is to relate the constraint to a superset of elements that contain the affected set and then to identify general principles that eliminate all of the unaffected elements of this superset. The second strategy makes sense when there is no obvious way to relate the constraint in question to the set of elements that are subject to it, which appears to be the case for *that*-trace effects. This is the approach Chomsky (1981) adopts when he proposes the Empty Category Principle (ECP). The ECP implements the idea that all empty categories are illegitimate elements in a sentences if nothing rescues them. This immediately ensures that sentences with empty categories in the subject position will be ungrammatical, so *that*-trace violations are covered. The question then becomes how to account for all the sentences in which empty categories do occur, so a set of exceptions—rescue operations— are proposed. Lexically governed empty categories are exempted, and so are antecedent-governed empty categories; see figure 5.1 in (5).

(5)

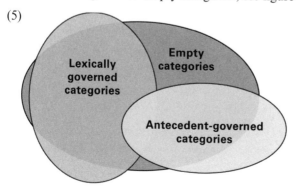

Whatever empty categories are not included in the exemptions will continue to ensure ungrammaticality in the ECP theory.

5.2.2 The Problem with Successive Cyclic Ā-Movement

Approaches based on the ECP ultimately fail empirically, because no satisfactory definitions of lexical and antecedent government succeed in isolating exactly the right class of empty categories that are permissible in grammatical sentences. But the strategy of explaining the *that*-trace effect by identifying a larger set of problematic structures is still a good one. Rather than trying to say why it is hard to move [Spec, Fin] categories from inside ForceP, then, let us consider what larger sets there might be that include the set of [Spec, Fin] categories. One obvious superset is the set of elements in Ā-positions. Is there any reason why Ā-categories might resist Ā-movement? If so, then a better explanation for *that*-trace effects may go like this: Successive cyclic Ā-movement is impossible generally, but there are rescue strategies or repair mechanisms that make it possible in specific contexts. None of the repair mechanisms happen to apply when [Spec, Fin] is extracted from ForceP.

(Rizzi (2003) and Rizzi and Shlonsky (2007) adopt the same heuristic strategy in trying to explain *that*-trace effects in terms of their Criterial Freezing principle. For them, subject extraction is problematic precisely because it involves disrupting a structure that has been created to express certain necessary semantics. But the arguments presented in chapter 4, which show that subjects and nonsubjects are both sometimes extracted from [Spec, Fin], provide ample evidence that the extraction of subjects from a dedicated subject position is not the real phenomenon that gives rise to *that*-trace effects. So even if the Criterial Freezing principle is largely correct, it appears not to be relevant to the problems being considered here.)

Now let me flesh out this scenario. Consider what successive cyclic Ā-movement produces, and what is required for interpretation at LF. Ā-chains must be transformed somehow into operator-variable chains for interpretation at the LF interface (Chomsky 1986b). The Refine operation accomplishes this. In the simplest case, Refine transforms three-member chains containing a probe into two member operator-variable structures, as in (6).

(6) ([which cat], Force, [which cat]) → ([which x], [x: cat(x)])

Successive cyclic Ā-movement takes structures that have already been refined and extends them, by adding a new probe and a new external match. Consider the derivation of sentence (7a), with the structure something akin to (7b). Let us suppose, temporarily, that movement is simply "Comp-to-Comp," and that vP phases are not obstacles to object movement.

(7) a. Whom should I say that Pam has invited?
    b. Whom^0 should I say whom^1 that Pam has invited whom^2?

Movement of *whom* from the object position to [Spec, Force] of the complement clause makes a copy of *whom*^{2}, and the chain that results is ternary, consisting of (*whom*^{1}, Force, *whom*^{2}). Chain refinement will then produce the usual operator-variable structure. So far, so good. But what happens when the [Spec, Force] *wh*-phrase is provoked? An external copy of the *wh*-phrase must be generated, but what does that mean for the number of chains and their constitution?

The immediate result will be a new chain structure containing the original elements of the earlier Ā-chain, together with the new Fin probe and the external wh-phrase: (*whom*^{0}, Fin, [wh x] ^{1}, [x: person(x)] ^{2}). And this new structure must then be processed by Refine. Refine eliminates the uninterpretable features from Fin, thereby removing the probe from the chain. And it must strip some of the content from the new *wh*-phrase, to create an operator. The only question is what happens to the rest of the chain—the elements that have already been processed by the earlier application of Refine.

There seem to be two alternatives. If Refine can access the products of earlier Refine operations, then it might potentially reduce them further, possibly eliminating the "intermediate trace" in the process. If this is the case, then successive cyclic movement is unproblematic, because successive applications of Refine may ensure that every Ā-chain becomes a valid operator-variable structure. Notice, however, that this conclusion comes at the cost of accepting a degree of redundancy in the derivation. Optimally, the Refine operation should be able to affect any item only once. If it needs to repair the effect of an earlier application, then the computation is performing extra work.

The other possibility is that Refine does nothing to the prerefined members of the chain. In that case, the result must be a chain that contains both the new operator and the operator formed when *wh*-movement took place in the complement clause. The chain will be (8).

(8) ([wh x] ^{0}, [wh x] ^{1}, [x: person(x)] ^{2})

Merge of the head of this chain into [Spec, Fin] then forms structure (9).

(9) wh x should I say [$_{\text{FcP}}$ wh x that Pam has invited x: person(x)]?

This is semantically incoherent. A single operator may be associated with multiple variables, but there is no conceivable interpretation for a single variable bound by multiple operators. Only the upper operator can be provided to the LF interface for interpretation in a successful derivation.

There is a second problem with the structure in (9). In the embedded clause, the *that* complementizer should be interpretable as a force marker, but force markers must be at the edge of their clause, and *that* is separated from the clause edge by a *wh*-phrase.

So the inefficient application of Refine ensures successive cyclic Ā-movement can occur, while the efficient application should make such movement impossible. At this point, we might simply conclude that inefficiency does not matter here, and that Refine can effectively eliminate intermediate traces in Ā-movement. But remember that we are trying to explain why successive cyclic movement actually fails sometimes. The *that*-trace effect is one of these cases of failed movement. If we instead embrace the conclusion that Refine applies efficiently, then we are one step closer to our goal.

5.2.3 Deletion by Force Markers

Let us suppose, then, that Refine cannot affect phrases that have already been processed. Then successive cyclic Ā-movement will be impossible, unless some other means can be identified to eliminate the toxic extra operators created by a second (or third, and so on) provocation operation.

Returning to sentences like (7a), with the structure (9), the problem the derivation imposes is that the trace in [Spec, Force] of the complement clause must be deleted. Since this sentence is actually grammatical, there must be a way to eliminate the intermediate trace in [Spec, Force]. The mechanism that accomplishes this must be fairly specific, since it will not do to have all traces deleted in a derivation, or all categories in [Spec, Force], either. For example, the *wh*-phrase in [Spec, Force] in (10), which will have semantic content identical to the trace in (9), must not be deleted.

(10) Should I say who Pam has invited?

If traces are not deleted immediately when chains are formed, then they probably should not be deleted in the narrow syntactic derivation at all. There is no other point in the derivation at which the *wh*-phrase itself is

As Bresnan (1976) observes, subject extraction from *for-to* infinitival complements is impossible in standard English.

(26) *Which guest did Jamie want badly for *t* to break the piñata?

The unacceptability of (26) is again due to the problem of too many operator-variable chains at the LF interface. Given the analysis of these structures in section 4.4, the subject raises from [Spec, T] to [Spec, Fin], just as it does in a finite clause. When the subject is provoked by the *for* Force head, the trace in [Spec, Fin] is not in a position where the CEIC can apply, so it is not deleted.

That-trace effects are also found in English with *if* complementizers, and in local *wh*-movement contexts:

(27) a.   *Who did they ask if had prepared the dinner?
     b. **Which printer do you know when is going on vacation?

With minor revisions, the explanation provided for pure *that*-trace violations will cover these cases as well.[2]

Although clearly monomorphemic, the *if* complementizer appears to play two roles: it signifies subordinate clause status, and it shows that the clause is a polar interrogative. It is plausible that these two roles involve two distinct positions in the left periphery. The subordinator function is similar to that of *that*, so should involve the Fin position; the interrogative force, on the other hand, should be identified with the Force head. At an abstract enough level, we might identify the initial structure of the complement clause in (28a) as (28b).

(28) a. Pam doesn't remember if the bus stops here.
     b. [$_{FcP}$ if- [$_{FinP}$ the bus -that [$_{TP}$ *t* stops here]]]

Like Force generally in asymmetric languages, the abstract *if*- complementizer is inherently defective because it lacks the subordinating force necessary to signal the full force of its clause. It must therefore attract *-that* from Fin to be complete, in a provocation operation that takes the closest [FORCE] bearing element as its goal. The result is (29).

(29) [$_{FcP}$ if-that [$_{FinP}$ the bus *e* [$_{TP}$ *t* stops here]]]

The surface form of abstract *if-that* is simply *if*.

Now consider the initial structure of the complement clause in the *if*-trace violation example (27a):

(30) [$_{FcP}$ if- [$_{FinP}$ who that [$_{TP}$ *t* had prepared the dinner]]]

Again, *if-* must provoke *-that* in order to serve as a complete force marker. But this time, the *wh*-phrase *who* is available to win the competition with *-that* as the best accessible goal for a [*u*FORCE] probe. So *who* is attracted to [Spec, Force], which is necessary in any case to allow it to escape from ForceP, and *-that* remains in Fin. The interpreted FinP at this point is the structure higher clause at the next phase level, the structure will be (31).

(31) [$_{\text{FinP}}$ wh x Fin [$_{\text{TP}}$ x: person(x) prepared the dinner]]

And once again, the absence of a force marker to its right means that the *wh*-phrase must be interpreted. The derivation therefore crashes.

The relatively weak subjacency violation that arises with object extraction from an *if* complement does not suffer from the same problem.

(32) ?Who did they ask if Peter would help?

It is evidently not fully permissible for *if* to provoke a *wh*-phrase. Overriding whatever principle prevents *if* from doing so results in a weak ungrammaticality judgment. But the trace left in [Spec, Force] when *who* is attracted into the matrix clause is still subject to deletion under CEIC, so (32) remains better than (27a).

Essentially the same account is available for the contrast between (27b) and (33).

(33) ??Which printer do you know when Tara will call?

The extraction of the object in (33) is blocked because the null head of ForceP cannot attract *which printer* to its edge. To the extent that this prohibition can be ignored, (33) is acceptable. But in (27b), where *which printer* must be raised from [Spec, Fin], there is the further and more serious problem that the intermediate Ā trace is not deleted by the CEIC, and the result is a stronger sense of unacceptability.

5.2.5 The "Adjunct" Effect

Culicover (1991) notes that the *that*-trace effect is weakened, and sometimes canceled out when certain adjuncts appear to the immediate right of the complementizer. For example, the presence of *just yesterday* in (34) rescues a sentence that would otherwise constitute a clear *that*-trace violation.

(34) ?Which car did Terry say that just yesterday had won the Indy?

Preposed arguments do not have the same effect (Culicover 1993). In fact, rather than improving the status of a sentence from which the subject is extracted, argument preposing makes it slightly worse.

(35) a. *Which car did Terry say that the Indy, had won?
     b. *Which car did Terry say that to Tonya, had been sold?

The effect of preposed arguments is not surprising in the present context. In (35b), *to Tonya* is topicalized to [Spec, Top], which produces an internal structure for the complement clause like (36).

(36) [FcP that [TopP [PP to Tonya] Top [FinP which car Fin [TP *t* had been sold *t*]]]]

Movement of *which car* from [Spec, Fin] to [Spec, Force] will leave the [Spec, Fin] trace intact; the clausal force marker is again to its left. A *that*-trace violation is expected here.

In fact, many adjuncts behave like fronted arguments in this respect. Haegeman (2003) shows that adjuncts that are construed in a lower clause than the one from which the subject is extracted are unable to cancel out the *that*-trace effect. Consider the (37) examples, where the adjunct *just yesterday* might in principle be understood either as predicated of the car-racing event in the bottom clause or as related to the thinking event in the second clause, but we are concerned only with the former construal.

(37) a. ??Beth said that *just yesterday* Peter thought that this car had
         won the Indy.
     b. *?Who did Beth say that *just yesterday* thought that this car had
         won the Indy?

In (37a), the adjunct *just yesterday* can marginally be construed as referring to the time of the race, rather than the time of Peter's thinking. But in (37b), where the subject of the middle clause is extracted, the adjunct can only be construed locally, as referring to the thinking time. If it is understood as referring to the time of the car race, the sentence is ungrammatical, as indicated.

Haegeman's treatment of this contrast is that adjuncts construed in a lower clause are found in the higher clause only by virtue of movement, while those construed locally are base-generated in the position where they appear. Thus, in (34), the adjunct *just yesterday* is merged into the position immediately after *that*, while in (37b), under the low construal reading, the adjunct is introduced initially into the bottom clause, and then raises into the left periphery of the matrix clause.

Haegeman's account, which I accept, fits naturally into the present theory. Topicalized arguments and adjuncts may be attracted by the P-feature of Top and raise to [Spec, Top]. The resulting structure in both cases will be (38).

(38)

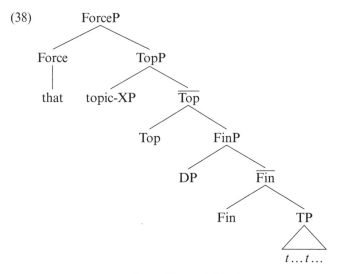

Subject extraction from [Spec, Fin] in any sentence with the (38) structure will inevitably leave an undeleted trace in [Spec, Fin], so the *that*-trace effect should be found here, just as it is in clauses with no topicalization. For example, (39), with the structure as shown, will occur in the derivation of (35a).

(39) [$_{FcP}$ wh x that [$_{TopP}$ the Indy Top [$_{FinP}$ wh x Fin [$_{TP}$ x: car(x) had won t]]]

But the [Spec, Fin] operator is neither at the edge of its clause nor adjacent to a force marker, so the CEIC does not apply. The sentence ends up with multiple operators for a single variable, and is therefore unacceptable.

The disappearance of *that*-trace effects when an appropriate adjunct is merged directly into a position to the right of *that* is more interesting, though hardly more difficult to explain. Recall from the discussion in section 3.3 that Fin may match some adverbials externally without requiring a simultaneous internal match with a copy of the same goal. There are therefore two ways for an adverbial to be fronted past the subject. For the adverbial to be "moved," it must bear a [TOPIC] feature and be provoked by Top. In that case, the structure will be equivalent to (38) in all relevant respects. However, if the adjunct is merged into [Spec, Fin] directly, then the ϕ-features of Fin are valued by the adverbial goal, and Fin cannot attract the subject up from [Spec, T]. With this type of derivation, the structure of the complement clause in (34) prior to subject *wh*-movement will be (40).

(40)

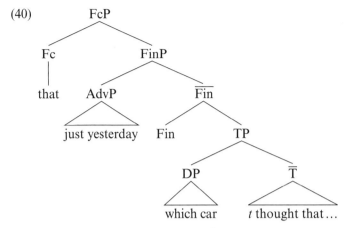

Since *which car* does not occupy an Ā-position, its trace does not need to be deleted when it later raises to [Spec, Force]. No *that*-trace violation is then possible with this structure.

As Culicover observes, subjects can be extracted even when a monotone-decreasing adjunct appears, in a verb-second structure.

(41) Which car did Tony say that at no earlier date had been entered in the race?

Here, of course, the adverbial again occupies [Spec, Fin]. It is again merged externally; no internal match is required to license it semantically. But the adverbial in this case values a provocative [MD] feature added to Fin, and not the ϕ-features. The latter must therefore provoke the auxiliary verb, which raises to Fin. Once again, the subject is left in its TP-internal position until Force attracts it. No intermediate trace is involved, so no *that*-trace effect can arise.

5.3 Crosslinguistic Variation

The pattern found in those dialects of English in which *that* appears as the head of a FinP complement clause are found elsewhere in the Germanic languages.

For many speakers of standard German, particularly in the north, successive cyclic *wh*-movement of the English variety is not possible at all. So object extraction and subject extraction are both barred, as shown in (42).

(42) *German* (Bayer 1984)
    a. *Wer glaubst du   daß *t* Emma liebt?
       who think   you that   Emma loves
       'Who do you think loves Emma?'

    b. *Wen glaubst du daß Emma *t* liebt?
       whom think   you that Emma loves
       'Who do you think that Emma loves?'

One might speculate that this is a language variety in which the CEIC does not apply at all, as a parametric option. In any case, it is clear that discussion of the presence or absence of a *that*-trace effect in this language is fruitless. However, the corresponding sentences in Bavarian German are grammatical.

(43) *Bavarian German* (Bayer 1984)
    a. Wer moanst du daß *t* d'Emma mog?
      who think   you that Emma loves
      'Who do you think loves Emma?'
    b. Weam moanst du daß d'Emma *t* mog?
      whom think   you that Emma   loves
      'Who do you think that Emma loves?'

Example (43a) shows that Bavarian German does not display pure *that*-trace effects. In this language variety, then, bare FinP may appear as a declarative complement with an overt *daß* complementizer as its head. A trace left in [Spec, Fin] can be ignored under the CEIC because it appears next to a force marker at the clause edge. The structure of (43a) will therefore be (44).

(44) [$_{FinP}$ wer moanst-Fin [$_{TP}$ du *e* [$_{FinP}$ wer daß [$_{TP}$ *t* d'Emma mog]]]]

    Much the same can be said of Dutch, although the data in this language are more controversial. Consider (45).

(45) *Dutch* (Koster 1987)
    a. Wie zei hij dat *t* Wim gezien had?
       who said he that   Bill seen   had
    b. ?Wie denk je   dat *t* verdwenen is?
       who think you that   disappeared is
    c. Wie denk je   dat *t* het gedaan heeft?
       who think you that it   dones has
      'Who do you think did it?'

In some Dutch sentences, such as (45b), subject extraction appears to degrade the acceptability. (Pesetsky (1982) maintains that extraction of the subject of some verbs is ungrammatical in Dutch.) But the degree of degradation is quite mild, as Koster (1987) points out, so it is unlikely that this can be attributed to the same principles that give rise to the (stronger) *that*-trace effect. Koster concludes that Dutch does not exhibit *that*-trace effects at all, and I accept his argument.

Dutch is a language in which bare FinP declarative complements can bear an overt complementizer: *dat*. The *dat* complementizer normally raises to Force, but when the subject is removed from the clause, ForceP cannot be present. So the structure of (45c) will be (46), and the subject trace in [Spec, Fin] is ignored under the CEIC, as in Bavarian German, French, and some dialects of English.

(46) [$_{FinP}$ wie denk-Fin [$_{TP}$ je [$_{FinP}$ wie dat [$_{TP}$ *t* het gedaan heeft?]]]]

The mainland Scandinavian languages offer a particularly intricate array of data for analysis of *that*-trace effects. These languages are grammatically uniform with respect to *that*-trace effects in embedded verb-second structures, but they vary considerably with non-verb-second complements. The Danish example (47) illustrates the general situation for subject extraction from embedded verb-second.[3]

(47) *Danish*
      *Hvilket æble   siger de   sagkundige [$_{FcP}$ *t* at   Top [$_{FinP}$ *t* smager
       which   apple say the   experts   that   tastes
       ikke bedst]]?
       not best

Although this superficially resembles a *that*-trace effect, and although the explanation developed for English *that*-trace effects could certainly be applied to this case as well, the ungrammaticality of (47) simply reflects the expected workings of an embedded verb-second structure. Since *at* in (47) is an abstractly incorporated complementizer, it cannot provoke the *wh*-phrase *hvilket æble* in [Spec, Fin], just as it cannot provoke any other *wh*-phrase. So the *wh*-phrase cannot be displaced to the edge of the ForceP phase, and the Phase Impenetrability Condition therefore rules the sentence out. The same is true for extraction of the initial constituent in embedded verb-second complements in the other Scandinavian languages.

Turning now to the non-verb-second complements, the comparative findings in the literature are as follows. In standard Swedish and Danish, *that*-trace effects are found with the declarative *at(t)* complementizer (Platzack 1986; Hellan and Christensen 1986).[4]

(48) *Swedish* (Holmberg 1986)
      *Vem sa   du   att *t* hade komit?
       who said you that   had arrived

In Swedish, subject extraction is possible when the complementizer is omitted, as in English. In Danish, there are two ways to permit the subject to escape: the complementizer may be omitted, as in Swedish, or an expletive *der* may be inserted to fill the Spec-FinP position. The latter strategy resembles the use of locally construed adjuncts in English, because the presence of *der* means that the subject itself never has to raise to [Spec, Fin], so no trace has to be deleted from [Spec, Fin]. Where the complementizer is missing, I suppose that a bare FinP complement is used, just as in the prevalent English dialect.

In Norwegian, and in Finnish-Swedish (Holmberg 1986), extraction past an overt complementizer is possible, as seen in the Norwegian question in (49a) and the long topicalization in (49b).

(49) *Norwegian* (Holmberg 2000)
    a. Hvem tror   du   (at) har stjalet sykkeken?
        who   think you that has stolen the-bike
        'Who do you think has stolen the bike?'
    b. (Hellan and Christensen 1986)
        Petter vet   jeg at   skal komme.
        Peter know I   that will come
        'Peter, I know that he will come.'

This dialectal variation in mainland Scandinavian can be treated along the same lines as in English. While standard Swedish does not permit *at* to function as the head of a bare FinP, Finnish Swedish does. The presence of *at* is enough to show that ForceP is a part of the complement clause in standard Swedish, but not in Finnish Swedish. And when ForceP is present, the subject trace in [Spec, Fin] cannot be deleted by the CEIC. But in Finnish Swedish, provocation of the *wh*-phrase produces the structure (50), in which the trace in [Spec, Fin] can be deleted.

(50) Fin du tror [_FinP_ vem at [_TP_ har stjalet sykkeken]]
                 vem

The *om* 'if' complementizer behaves differently. *Om* blocks subject extraction in standard Swedish, but not in Danish, Finnish Swedish, or Norwegian. The contrast between Swedish, on the one hand, and Norwegian and Danish, on the other, is seen in (51).

(51) a. *Swedish* (Engdahl 1984)
        *Kalle kan man aldrig vara säker på om *t* dykker upp.
        Kalle can one never be   sure on if   shows up

    b. *Danish*
       Det ved   jeg ikke om *t* gaar an.
       that know I   not if   is   allowed
    c. *Norwegian*
       Hvem visste du ikke om hadde skrevet boken?
       who knew you not if had   written book-the
       'Who did you not know if he had written the book?'

This contrast calls for a different type of crosslinguistic variation, one in which the position of the polar interrogative complementizer is variable. The examination of English embedded verb-second interrogatives in section 4.3 concludes that verbs like *ask* permit an interrogative clausal complement that does not include a ForceP projection in some English dialects. The sentences in example (110) in chapter 4 (repeated here) reprise some of McCloskey's (2007) illustrations of this phenomenon.

(110) a. Sheila was wondering [$_{TopP}$ when she finishes work [$_{FinP}$ where should-Fin [$_{TP}$ she meet us *t t*]]].
      b. I wonder [$_{TopP}$ when you get home [$_{FinP}$ if [$_{TP}$ we should order pizza *t*]]].

In this construction, either the *if* complementizer or a null head that provokes the auxiliary verb may be generated in Fin. When *if* is used in the Fin position, though, it behaves like the cognate Force head in one important respect. Unlike the null Fin in (51a), *if* lacks provocative ϕ-features; it attracts neither the auxiliary verb nor the subject from within TP.

    Norwegian and Danish do not permit embedded interrogatives with inverted word order, but the data in (51) indicate that they do permit the *om* polar complementizer to be realized in the Fin position, if the matrix context is one that licenses the omission of ForceP. (This must evidently be a marked situation crosslinguistically, given the rarity of structures like these in other languages, so we would expect to find positive evidence in the linguistic environment of Danish or Norwegian children.) One Norwegian informant informs me that the acceptability of subject extraction past *om* or a *wh*-phrase improves substantially if the matrix clause is negated, as well as with an auxiliary verb in the complement clause.[5] The improved status of subject extraction with matrix negators might then be because matrix negators encourage the use of bare FinP complements, with the force marker in Fin.[6] In (51c), for example, the presence of the negator *ikke* in the matrix clause licenses a bare FinP interrogative complement, so the structure is (52).

(52) [$_{TopP}$ denne boken Top [$_{FinP}$ t husker-Fin [$_{TP}$ jeg ikke [$_{FinP}$ om [$_{TP}$ t er oversatt til norsk]]]]]

With this specific feature complex in place, the mechanism for subject extraction will be the same as that for object extraction, since both subjects and objects will be attracted directly from within TP. No problem can arise concerning an undeleted trace in [Spec, Fin] because the subject will not be attracted to [Spec, Fin] by *om* at any point in the derivation.

Danish and Norwegian take this distinction one step further. In these languages, subject extraction is even allowed from within indirect *wh*-questions (Taraldsen 1986a), as illustrated by (53).

(53) a. Han spurte hvem du   ikke visste nar   hadde skrevet boken?
        he asked who you not knew when had   written book-the
        'He asked who you didn't know when he had written the book.'

     b. *Norwegian* (Engdahl 1984)
        Denne boken husker   jeg ikke når t ble oversatt   til
        this   book remember I   not when   was translated into
        norsk.
        Norwegian

     c. *Norwegian*
        Denne forfattaren husker   jeg ikke hva t har oversatt t til
        this   author   remember I   not what   has translated   to
        norsk.
        Norwegian

     d. *Danish*
        De tjente en mann som de   ikke hviste hvem t var t.
        they served a man that they not knew   who   was

Once again, the matrix contexts are those that license a bare FinP interrogative complement. In this case, instead of polar *om*, the complementizer that occupies the Fin position is the null element that attracts *wh*-phrases. Like *om*, the null complementizers in (53) lack a provocative ϕ-feature complex, so the subject is not displaced from [Spec, T]. Subject extraction into the matrix clause is therefore unproblematic.[7]

As we see, Norwegian and Danish allow bare FinP complements in a wider set of contexts than Swedish does, and greater potential for subject $\bar{\text{A}}$-movement is then possible in these languages. When the context excludes bare FinP in any Scandinavian language, then subject extraction is uniformly constrained. This is the case in relative clauses in which the relative pronoun originates in a nonsubject position. Engdahl (1984) observes that extraction of the subject is always impossible from this configuration:

(54) *Norwegian* (Hellan and Christensen 1986)
    *Petter finner vi ikke den boken som t har skrevet t.
    Peter find   we not the book that has written
    'Peter, we don't find the book that he has written.'

As usual in relative clauses, ForceP must be present to provide a landing site for the silent relative pronoun in (54). Fin, too, has the properties elucidated in section 4.1: *som* originates in Fin and is provoked by Force, which can then go on to provoke the relative pronoun. Fin bears provocative ϕ-features, so the subject raises to [Spec, Fin]. As a result, any subsequent Ā-movement of the subject will need to be accompanied by deletion of the trace from [Spec, Fin]. But the CEIC does not exempt the [Spec, Fin] trace in the configuration found in (54), so extraction of *Petter* is impossible.

    In Icelandic, a symmetric verb-second language, the subject extraction pattern is similar to that of Finnish Swedish. Subject extraction is possible with the declarative *það* complementizer, but not from within indirect questions.

(55) *Icelandic* (Rögnvaldsson 1984)
    Sveinn veit ég að   hefur lesið bókina.
    Sveinn know I that has read the   book
    'I know that Sveinn has read the book.'

(56) *Icelandic* (Maling and Zaenan 1978)
    a. Hvaða bragð sagði hann að *t* vaeri gagnslaust?
       which deed said he   that   was useless
    b. Þetta er maþurinn, sem þeir segja að *t* hafi framið
       this is the-man that they say   that has committed
       glæpinn.
       the-crime
    c. Þetta sverð heldur konungurinn að *t* sé galdrasverð.
       this sword thinks the-king   that is magic-sword

Although Icelandic allows expletive *pro* in embedded questions, Maling and Zaenen show that expletives cannot be used to make subject extraction possible. It follows that the extracted subjects in (56) must raise to [Spec, Fin] of the complement clause at some point in the derivation. The only way for the [Spec, Fin] trace to be deleted under the CEIC is then if *að* occupies Fin in these sentences, so that ForceP is not present.

This result may seem problematic, since complementizers must normally originate in Force in Icelandic. In fact, though, there is no contradiction. Whenever ForceP is present, Force is the location where a complementizer must originate. When Force contains a complementizer, Fin cannot contain one too, since complementizers must appear at the edge of their clause. So Fin is usually a null affix, and must therefore usually attract the finite verb. But bare FinP is permitted in Icelandic in the same conditions as it is permitted in other languages, and with no complementizer present in Force, Fin may then contain *að*, as long as subsequent subject extraction leaves the complementizer at the clause edge.

It appears to be the case that bare FinP complements provide the context in which Icelandic stylistic fronting is permitted. Simply as a descriptive generalization, stylistic fronting appears to be a process that adjoins a head other than the finite verb to Fin, when Fin is not the null affix.

(57) Þennan mann hélt   ég [$_{FinP}$ að-farið [$_{TP}$ *t* hefði verið *t* med *t* á
       this   man thought I   that-gone   had been   with to
       sjúkrahús]]
       hospital

5.4   A Spooky Constraint

The CEIC allows us to understand a second, less familiar, constraint on Ā-movement, which can be detected in German, and in the Belfast dialect of English documented by Henry (1995).

5.4.1   Successive Cyclic Inversion
In German, inverted word order can be triggered by successive cyclic Ā-movement, as in (58).

(58) In zwei wochen glaubt   Anna, [$_{FinP}$ *t* hat Max gesagt, [$_{FinP}$ *t* werde
      in two weeks   believes Anna   has Max said   will
      sie *t* kommen.]]
      she come
      'Anna believes Max said she will come in two weeks.'

The same type of movement is permitted in the derivation of questions. Successive cyclic inversion is possible because long *wh*-movement in German can make use of [Spec, Fin] as an escape hatch from a lower clause. Thus in (59), the *wh*-phrase *wann* raises from the edge of a verb-second complement clause into the matrix clause.

pear at the left edge of a clause, so the possibility of Fin being used in this way will be contingent on extraction of the specifier of Fin to a higher position.

Consider the structures interpreted at the LF interface in the derivation of (65a). Since FinP is not phasal, everything external to the vP phases is presented for LF interpretation at once:

(70) [$_{FinP}$ wh x did John [$_{vP}$ ...] [$_{FinP}$ wh x would he [$_{vP}$ ...]]]

With the lower Fin understood as a force marker at the edge of its clause, CEIC now allows the intermediate trace to be ignored, and the derivation can converge.

But now we must consider the ungrammatical successive inversion cases anew. If intermediate traces in [Spec, Fin] are always subject to CEIC, then what accounts for the ungrammaticality of (65c)?

It seems that the latitude that we are allowed in interpreting Fin as a force marker is sensitive to the sentential context. If there is an actual complementizer—or its zero interrogative analog—present at the point at which the CEIC is relevant, then a verb-attracting Fin head cannot be taken to be a force marker. In other words, Fin is allowed to function as a force marker only when the context does not provide a better example of what a force marker should look like.

In (65c), when the ForceP phase is presented to LF, the structure will be (71).

(71) [$_{FcP}$ who that John [$_{vP}$ ...] who would-Fin Bill [$_{vP}$ ...]]]

And the presence of the *that* complementizer in this phase ensures that the lower Fin cannot count as a force marker for CEIC. The lower intermediate trace is thus interpreted, and the derivation crashes.

The same explanation is available for the German (62). Again, the problem must be that the intermediate trace in [Spec, Fin] of the lowest embedded clause is not deleted. And the explanation is that the phase in which deletion should take place will contain a better example of a force marker, so the CEIC cannot apply.

(72) [$_{FcP}$ wh x ∅ ihnen Fritz [$_{vP}$ ...] hat [$_{FinP}$ wh x werde-Fin sie x: Zeit(x) komen]]]

In Yiddish, both types of successive cyclic movement are freely available, so Yiddish provides a clear demonstration of how the CEIC interacts with context to produce a complex set of superficial extraction constraints.

(73) *Yiddish* (Diesing 1990)

    a.   Vos hot er nit gevolt az   mir zoln   leyenen *t*?
        what has he not wanted that we should read
        'What did he not want us to read?'

    b.   Vos hot er nit gevolt zoln   mir leyenen *t*?
        what has he not wanted should we read

    c. *Vos hot er nit gevolt az   zoln   mir leyenen *t*?
        what has he not wanted that should we read

    d. *Vos hot er nit gevolt mir zoln   leyenen *t*?
        what has he not wanted we should read

    e. ?Vos hot er nit gevolt az es zoln   mir leyenen *t*?
        what has he not wanted that ES should we read

(74) a.   Ven hostu   gezogt az   Max hot geleyent dos bukh *t*?
        when have-you said   that Max has read   the book
        'When did you say that Max read the book?'

    b.   Ven   hostu   gezogt hot Max geleyent dos bukh?
        when have-you said   has Max read   the book

    c. *Ven hostu   gezogt Max hot geleyent dos bukh?
        when have-you said   Max has read   the book

    d. *Ven hostu   gezogt az   hot Max geleyent dos bukh?
        when have-you said   that has Max read   the book

Examples (73a) and (74a) are cases of familiar successive cyclic *wh*-movement of nonsubjects. Movement of the *wh*-phrases through [Spec, Force] produces traces that can be deleted by the CEIC. In the (73b) and (74b) sentences, the complement clause is a bare FinP and the *wh*-phrases are raised from a lower [Spec, Fin] to a higher [Spec, Fin] position. Since there are no Force/complementizer heads in these structures, the verb-attracting Fin is permitted to function as a force marker, and the CEIC therefore allows the problematic intermediate traces to be deleted.

Examples (73c) and (74d) resemble *that*-trace effects, but what is extracted is not the subject.[9] However the principles that exclude this type of sentence are the same. Since the complementizer *az* is present (and Yiddish is a symmetric verb-second language), the complement clause is a ForceP category. The *wh*-phrases must therefore escape *via* the [Spec, Force] phrasal escape hatch. But movement from [Spec, Fin] to [Spec, Force] requires the generation of structures like (75).

(75) [$_{FcP}$ az [$_{FinP}$ wh x Fin [$_{TP}$ . . . x . . .]]]
            wh x

The CEIC cannot delete the [Spec, Fin] trace in (75) because it is not outside a force marker. Two many operators are present in the LF mapping, and the derivation crashes.

The unacceptability of the (73d) and (74c) examples does not involve a problem of trace deletion, since no extraction from [Spec, Fin] takes place. Instead, these are simple violations of the Phase Impenetrability Condition. As established in section 4.3, Yiddish embedded verb-second clauses with no visible complementizer always involve incorporation of the null Force head by the matrix verb. But incorporation of Force makes it unable to provoke a *wh*-phrase, so *vos* and *ven* cannot escape from the ForceP island.

Finally, the marginal (73e) is possible with the expletive pronoun *es* occupying [Spec, Fin]. Again, no trace deletion problem arises within FinP, because the object is provoked by Force in its original position within TP.

Pure *that*-trace effects also arise in Yiddish, as in (76).

(76) a. *Ver hot er moyre az vet kumen?
    who has he fear that will come
    'Who is he afraid will come?'
  b. Ver hot er moyre vet kumen?
    who has he fear will come
  c. ?Ver hot er moyre az es vet kumen?
    who has he fear that ES will come

These structures pose no new problems. The ungrammatical (76a) reflects movement from [Spec, Fin] to [Spec, Force], like (73c) and (74d). But the CEIC prohibits deletion of the [Spec, Fin] trace. In the derivation of (76b), though, matrix Fin provokes the *wh*-phrase directly in the lower [Spec, Fin] position, so the trace can be deleted. And the use of the expletive *es* in [Spec, Fin] in (76c) permits the subject to be extracted directly from [Spec, T], so that no trace deletion rule is necessary to rescue the structure. In this respect, example (76c) is comparable to the English sentences discussed in section 5.2, in which the introduction of an adjunct into [Spec, Fin] cancels out the expected *that*-trace effect. In Yiddish, however, even argument topicalization can produce the same result, as seen in (77).

(77) (Diesing 1990)
    Ver hot er nit gevolt az ot di bikher zol leyenen?
    who has he not wanted that the books should read
    'Who did he not want to read the books?'

This pattern is to be expected, since Yiddish allows embedded verb-second order even when Force is not incorporated by a matrix predicate. The *az* complementizer can still provoke the subject *ver* inside TP after the object is attracted to [Spec, Fin], and to [Spec, Top]. So the Phase Impenetrability Condition is satisfied, and no trace deletion problem arises in (77).

5.5 Short *Wh*-Movement in Embedded Questions

Of necessity, *that*-trace effects arise only when Ā-movement spans more than one clause. However, given the analysis of inversion structures presented in chapters 3 and 4, the same issues will sometimes arise even with Ā-movement within a single clause. Since subjects normally occupy [Spec, Fin]—an Ā-position—*wh*-movement of subjects in embedded clauses is now potentially problematic.

Consider (78).

(78) Bob enquired which desperado had pitched this tent.

Since Fin must provoke the subject to value its ϕ features, the subject raises to [Spec, Fin]. And embedded questions include a Force head that attracts a *wh*-phrase, so the same *wh*-phrase must raise to [Spec, Force]. The result should be the structure (79) for the embedded question in (78).

(79) $[_{FcP}$ wh x Fc $[_{FinP}$ wh x Fin $[_{TP}$ x: desperado(x) had pitched this tent]]]

But with two operators present, there can be no successful LF interpretation of this structure.

Fortunately, the CEIC provides the means to allow for this structure to converge. It is clear that the lower operator phrase in (79) cannot be ignored at LF because it does not appear to the left of any force marker. (Fin cannot be a force marker here because it is not at the edge of its clause.) But the upper operator *is* in the right position to be ignored. There is a potential force marker to its right. And deletion of the upper *wh*-phrase will not leave the clause without its *wh*-operator, since the operator in [Spec, Fin] will remain available for interpretation.

This strategy is obviously not available in the case of long-distance movement. Movement of a *wh*-phrase into a higher clause will typically take place only because the scopal and selectional requirements of the sentence demand that this takes place. But if the operator is deleted from its new position in a higher clause, then nothing remains to deliver the right interrogative semantics. So deletion of the upper operator in successive cyclic Ā-movement structures will naturally be restricted to very local movement cases.

But sometimes even when local *wh*-movement takes place, something reminiscent of the *that*-trace effect is found. Consider the Yiddish data in (80) (from Diesing 1990), for example.

(80) Ikh veys nit ver   *(es) is gekumen.
     I   know not who   it   is come
     'I know who came.'

Without the expletive *es*, short *wh*-movement of the subject is impossible in Yiddish. This cannot be explained as a result of the creation of too many operators, since the upper operator in Yiddish should be just as readily deleted as it must be in English. Instead, the ungrammaticality of (80) (without the expletive) must reflect some language-particular property of this language.

I suspect that the problem is with the Force head in Yiddish embedded questions. Recall that Force will normally attract Fin in any noninverting embedded clause in which the [Spec, Fin] subject is not provoked instead. (See section 4.2 for the details.) Suppose that Yiddish interrogative Force needs to provoke Fin in every case. In other words, the Yiddish interrogative Force head is affixal, and must be supported by attracting a lower head. In any question where the *wh*-phrase does not occupy [Spec, Fin], Force will provoke Fin after it attracts the *wh*-phrase to serve as its specifier. But when the subject is both a *wh*-phrase and as close as the Fin is as a potential goal for Force, the subject must be provoked instead. And then Force cannot attach to another supporting head.

The obligatory insertion of *es* in (80) can now be seen as a strategy to keep the subject from raising to [Spec, Fin] so that it cannot compete with Fin as a goal for the Force probe. Force can therefore provoke the subject simply as a *wh*-phrase, and it can attract Fin to lend it the morphological support it requires.

Yiddish also employs adjuncts to allow short *wh*-movement of the subject to take place, as in (81).

(81) (Diesing 1990)
     ... vi ikh veys vos   bay mir tut   zikh
         as I   know what by   me does itself
     '... as I know what goes on with me'

As with *es*-insertion, the effect of inserting the adverbial *bay mir* directly into [Spec, Fin] in (81) is that Force can continue to provoke Fin without the subject getting in the way.

5.6 Conclusion

To sum up, if we assume that movement involves the formation of distinct copies of an original phrase, it is possible to formulate a comprehensive account of phenomena like *that*-trace effects. The Clause Edge Interpretation Convention is a plausible rule with considerable coverage, which can only apply to structures formed by chain formation processes that do produce multiple copies of a phrase in motion. If we reject the idea that movement has this character, then no explanation of this type is formulable. And to the extent that other analyses of this particular type of limitation on phrasal movement are lacking, we are then left without any explanation at all of some very common grammatical phenomena. Embracing the idea that movement forms multiple copies seems worthwhile.

At this point, two conclusions can be drawn. The first is narrow and technical. The theory of movement described in chapter 2 is based on a conception of chain formation in which two separate categories are joined by the valuation operation into one complex unit. The components of a chain nevertheless maintain their individual identities in several respects. It is the idea that the members of a chain are distinct units that makes it possible to describe successive cyclic movement as a derivational path that will naturally produce uninterpretable chain structures—structures that always contain too many operators. And this treatment of successive cyclic movement then provides a natural account of phenemena like *that*-trace effects, in all their crosslinguistic glory, and like the peculiar spooky constraint that controls long movement in German and Belfast English. No account with comparable coverage has previously been offered in the literature.

The second conclusion is more general. The picture of the syntactic derivation that emerges from this discussion is relatively complex. The elementary operations that go into normal syntactic derivations include all of the list in (82).

(82) *Elementary derivational operations*
Match
Valuation
Refine
Merge
Transfer

We might ask at this point whether this model is really "minimal," in Chomsky's (1993, 3) sense. Do these ideas add up to a "theory of language that takes a linguistic expression to be nothing other than a formal object that satisfies the interface conditions in the optimal way"?

For a portion of this list, the answer is certainly yes. The Merge and Transfer operations are clearly inescapable in any theory of human language, and it is difficult to imagine how they could be optimized further. And the Match operation simply names a minimal search algorithm, which also seems to fit into an optimal computational design. Of course, I have taken these operations into my model from the existing minimalist literature, so there is little advantage to establishing their "minimalist" credentials.

What is left to evaluate are the Refine and Valuation operations. Refine is the easier of the two, because it simply anticipates within the derivation what some of the needs of the interface might be. In that respect, it too seems optimal. Given that the interface will always impose some requirements on the output of the syntactic derivation, a mechanism to try to satisfy those requirements ahead of time is a valuable—optimal—component of the computational machinery.

We are left with the Valuation operation. It is clear that natural language does include some mechanism for feature dependencies to be established within a phrase marker. Agreement is real, after all. And treating agreement as feature sharing seems to add no real complexity to the basic phenomenon. But the answer to the larger question of whether Valuation is a natural part of good design principles remains elusive. What the provocation model contributes to this question is simply a clearer picture of *why* Valuation is a necessary part of accomplishing whatever syntactic movement tries to achieve. Valuation forms chains, so it is a way of adding another dimension to phrase markers, thereby allowing the Ā-system to express a range of ideas that only chain formation makes possible.

So Valuation is clearly a handy component of the computational system. Is it optimal? At this point, my own intuitions about where to look for an answer begin to crash, so I have to leave it to others to work out what we should look for here.

Notes

Chapter 1

1. Epstein and Seely (2006) provide an exhaustive critique of the empirical justifications for the EPP. Their central concern is the status of the [Spec, T] position, however, rather than the role of the EPP or EPP features in driving movement. For the most part, the issues that concern them are orthogonal to those discussed here.

2. The literature on the EPP also includes various proposals to associate the subject position with a particular semantic role having something to do with clausal "aboutness." Such theories are not vulnerable to the charge of circularity. Notable contributions in this area include Rothstein 1983 and Rizzi 2003. To my mind, approaches of this type have not surmounted the general problem that the subject position sometimes seems to be entirely lacking in special semantics, as when expletive subjects are used. Rizzi (2003) disagrees.

3. Chomsky (2008, 8) observes: "It has sometimes been supposed that a new 'copy' is created, then inserted in the position of the moved element—all unnecessary—and an alternative has been proposed in terms of 'remerge,' which is simply the copy theory as originally formulated."

Chapter 2

1. The provocation theory developed here is informed by earlier proposals on "sideward movement" by Nunes (2004). In Nunes's work, as in mine, movement creates sets of independent phrase markers that are subsequently unified by a merge operation. The primary goal of the two models is quite different, however, as is the implementation of this shared conception. For Nunes, movement is still driven by the EPP, even if the components of the complex movement operation do not satisfy the EPP immediately. And he maintains that "copies" are derived from the original phrase marker, while I derive the notion of a copied element indirectly, from the feature valuation process, as described in section 2.2. It remains an open question to what extent these two approaches might benefit from unification.

2. By hijacking Chomsky's (2000) terminology, I do mean to imply that provocative features will do the work of Chomsky's P-features, or Chomsky's (2008) "edge features."

3. One might imagine that a copy of the goal feature (set) alone would satisfy the demands of a provocative probe, and this might be allowed in principle. But subsequent introduction of the bare features into the original phrase marker will not produce a valid, interpretable output, so such a derivation must fail on other grounds.

4. The question does not arise in Rizzi's own model, which starts from slightly different assumptions about the forces that drive *wh*-movement.

5. An anonymous reviewer points out that the same argument might be made for regular polar questions, which presumably are formed with a null interrogative operator merged (externally) at the root. The claim would again be that interrogative C matches its unvalued feature against this type of external goal. On the other hand, Larson (1985) has argued that polar questions are formed by *movement* of a disjunction operator from a TP-internal position. If Larson is correct, then the text analysis of *perché* cannot be extended in this way.

6. The implication here, as in Chomsky's analysis, is that *there* must bear some ϕ-feature or feature set. This is necessary in any theory in which agreement and movement are connected, since *there* can certainly undergo raising, in sentences like (i).

(i) There seemed to be believed to be several ships in the harbor.

7. The agreement in finite clauses between T and the "associate" of *there* can be accommodated even if T never conducts a second search after *there* is merged. Since ϕ-feature complexes are shared after agreement takes place, the features of *there* are shared with T whenever *there* fills the subject position. But the features of *there* may themselves be mutable. Suppose that *there* must find a value for *some* portion of its own ϕ-features by a valuation operation. Then *there* must act as a probe and conduct a search within the clause for the closest element that has a match for the unvalued features. The match will be the indefinite nominal within the verb phrase, the features of which are thereafter shared with *there*. And since *there* already shares its ϕ-features with T, the features of the associate will automatically be shared with T, too.

8. The central argument for feature sharing in Frampton and Gutmann 2000 is quite simple and persuasive. Consider the Icelandic data in (i)–(v), taken from Andrews 1982.

(i) Hún   er vinsæl.
    she-NOM is popular

(ii) Þeir   segja hana   vera vinsæla.
     they-NOM say   her-ACC to-be popular

(iii) Hún   er sögð   vera vinsæl.
      she-NOM is said-NOM to-be popular

(iv) Þeir   telja   hana   vera sagða   vera vinsæla.
     they-NOM believe her-ACC to-be said-ACC to-be popular

(v) Hún   er talin   vera sögð   vera vinsæl.
     she-NOM is believed-NOM to-be said-NOM to-be popular

The passive participles in each example agree in Case with the *hún/hana* pronoun. But the Case of that pronoun is not determined until it has raised past the participle to a higher position in the sentence, or even several clauses up. In (v), for example, the pronoun is assigned nominative Case by T in the root clause after it has raised from its original clause through an intermediate clause. And there is no reason to suppose that root T has any direct checking/valuation relationship with the participle two clauses down.

If valuation is feature sharing, then this pattern follows directly. Each participle may agree locally with the pronoun *hún/hana* before it raises out of the relevant clause, and the result of each agreement operation is that the shared ϕ-feature complex appears in one extra position. When Case is eventually assigned to the pronoun, it is automatically realized in each position where the shared features appear, which includes the pronoun itself and all heads that it has agreed with earlier in the derivation.

9. Poletto and Pollock (2004) describe the small interrogative pronouns in several Italian dialects in similar terms, as clitic elements, and the analysis of *wh*-clitics presented here seems appropriate for these languages as well.

10. I attribute the fact that *n*-intrusion does not occur in root clauses to the different positions occupied by *wh*-phrases in embedded clauses and root clauses in Germanic generally, as discussed in chapter 4. Small *wh*-words in south German are clitics only when they are attracted by the Force head, which triggers *wh*-movement in embedded clauses only.

11. In fact, bare subject pronouns are also clitic elements (Kayne 1975), but they cliticize to Fin rather than to T, as discussed in section 3.3.

12. The question remains open why T does not permit multiple specifiers in French. One possibility is that T actually does allow multiple (nonclitic) specifiers, but that only the outermost specifier is subject to PF interpretation. The true structure of a sentence like (38c) would then be (i).

(i) [$_{TP}$ Marc de Joanne les a emprunté...]

All other specifiers would instead be spelled-out at the foot of the chain. Pesetsky (2000) develops a model of English multiple-*wh* questions along these lines. But because I see no way at present to test the validity of this hypothesis, I do not pursue this line of analysis.

13. Krapova and Cinque (2008, 173 n. 2) suggest that this freedom is limited, but do not offer a thorough description or analysis of what the limitations are. At least some of the examples of free variation in the ordering of second and subsequent *wh*-phrases seem uncontroversially to be acceptable.

14. The Person-Case Constraint observed by Bonet (1991) is evidently relevant only to provocation of nonsubject clitics. It is plausible that this will be a consequence of the fact that T is valued by, and assigns Case to, only the first nominal that it provokes.

15. Stowell ensured this result with a *Case Resistance Principle*, which forced clauses to avoid occupying Case-marked position.

16. Chomsky (2008) locates the moment of valuation of unvalued features at the phase level, so that valuation and feature deletion will always be essentially simultaneous. In multiple *wh*-movement derivations, where a single probe must reuse the same features to drive further movement, it is difficult to maintain that valuation and feature deletion will always coincide. A more natural interpretation of the order of events in this scenario is suggested by the theory of Distributed Morphology (Halle and Marantz 1993), in which feature valuation can be said to provide the information necessary to calculate the morphological form of a feature complex. For sentences like (37b), for example, the initial valuation of the [uWH] feature of C would establish that the correct form must be a zero morpheme; subsequent operations involving the same probe would leave this morphological form intact. Full Spell-Out—which presumably occurs when the phase is complete—can then deal with the morphological content of C in the same way as it deals with any other morphemes in the phase.

17. Chomsky (2007, 2008) maintains, in addition, that both valuation and Transfer must always take place at the phase level. But the data discussed in chapter 4 seem to render the idea that everything happens at the phase level untenable.

18. The preference for specifiers might be attributed to the "extension condition" (Chomsky 1995). The use of head movement as a fallback solution may then fall together with the "tucking in" procedure adopted in languages with multiple specifier attraction (Richards 1997).

19. Bošković (1999) discusses several more opaque cases of a head attracting multiple other heads.

20. See also Zwart 2001 for critical evaluation of Chomsky's position.

21. Collins (2002) provides a particularly elegant demonstration of the close syntactic parallels between phrasal movement and head movement.

Chapter 3

1. Earlier proposals to the same effect include Culicover 1991, Branigan 1992, and Shlonsky 1994. Other labels that arguably identify the same position in a sentence include Culicover's PolP, ΣP (Laka 1990), as well as Agr$_S$ P (Belletti 1990; Chomsky 1993; Zwart 1997), under some interpretations. The Rizzian terminology has the advantage of a wider currency in the recent literature.

2. This whole approach to English auxiliary inversion is derived—with some important differences—from Pesetsky and Torrego's analysis of inversion in English root questions, in fact. Provocation aside, the important difference in the present analysis involves how subjects are analyzed in noninverted clauses.

3. Pesetsky (2000, 7–8) provides discussion relevant for this issue.

4. See also Kayne 1989b and Zwart 1997 for additional evidence for a "higher" subject position than [Spec, T].

5. Dutch topicalizations optionally include what appear to be resumptive pronouns in [Spec, Fin], as in (i).

(i) *Dutch* (Zwart 1997)
    Marie (die)   denk ik dat Jan gekust heeft.
    Marie that-one think I   that John kissed has
    'Mary I think that John kissed.'

Data like this might lead one to adopt Koster's (1978) proposal that normal topicalization involves a base-generated topic and a silent fronted operator. In terms of the model presented here, this would involve an operator preposed to [Spec, Fin] (provoked by the [MD] or [M̄D̄] feature) and a topic base-generated in [Spec, Top]. English locative inversion might then fall into place with structure (ii), with an optional null variant of *there* allowed in [Spec, Fin] when a locative antecedant appears in [Spec, Top].

(ii) [$_{TopP}$ in the jungle [$_{FinP}$ (there$_i$) Fin [$_{TP}$ t_i slept the lion]]]

Nothing central to my argument is affected by the choice between this alternative and the text analysis, so I leave the Kosterian variant as an unexplored possibility.

6. But see section 4.3 for discussion of dialectal English variants in which examples almost like (39b) appear acceptable.

7. More precisely, the constraint in (42) serves as the starting point in developing a set of optimality-theoretic constraints that govern the position of the verb in these dialects. The details are less important than the generalization for my purposes.

8. In examples like (i) and (ii), I assume the adverbial phrase *trots allt* is adjoined to TP.

(i) *Swedish* (Schwartz and Vikner 1996)
    Vill trots   allt Johan inte läsa de   här bökerna?
    will despite all Johan no   read these here books

(ii) De   här bökerna vill trots   allt Johan inte läsa.
     these here books   will despite all Johan not read

9. When Fin hosts an adverb in this way, it does much of the work that Rizzi (2004) ascribes to a separate Mod head.

10. It is significant that the affixal requirements of Fin are not sufficient to override the EPP preference for a specifier over a raised head. In effect, an uneconomical derivation is preferred to the economical alternative. This peculiarity may be taken as evidence that the verb movement seen in subject-initial verb-second clauses truly is a stylistic PF operation, and therefore excluded from considerations of derivational economy.

Chapter 4

1. There are two broad subtypes within the Germanic languages: the symmetric verb-second languages, which include Icelandic and Yiddish, and the asymmetric

verb-second languages, which include almost all the others. Despite not being a true verb-second language, English patterns with the symmetric verb-second languages in some respects.

2. Pesetsky and Torrego (2000) suggest a comparable type of variation distinguishes English from Spanish, with *that* originating in T in English, but *que* in C in Spanish.

3. Exceptions to this Spell-Out condition include Dutch *dat*, which can be interpreted to the right of other material in the left periphery. It cannot, however, appear to the right of something in [Spec, Fin].

4. Holmberg and Platzack (2005) ensure this same result for Icelandic in a similar fashion. For them, Icelandic Fin bears a [uPERSON] feature that attracts the finite verb in all clauses.

5. Zwart's (1993) approach also relies on the complementizer to support the head that is the locus of verb-second order—for him, that head is AgrS—and it is therefore able to cope with the asymmetric coordination data along the same lines as I suggest here. In fact, this is Zwart's analysis in a new guise.

6. This is essentially the proposal of Zwart 1993.

7. Roberts supposes that English *that* originates in Force and German *daß*, in Fin. A more nuanced typology of how complementizers are distributed across these two positions is developed here.

8. An anonymous reviewer observes that provocative ϕ-features on Force would trigger movement of the [Spec, Fin] subject, rather than of Fin itself. There is no evidence that ϕ-features are ever present on Force, though, so this situation should not arise. What is more, since movement of the subject to the [Spec, Force] position would typically usurp the edge position from the force-marking complementizer, there will be a natural resistance to Force ever acquiring ϕ-features in the first place.

9. Kim (2008) exploits this same basic idea to ensure that the *that* complementizer is pronounced in subject relative clauses.

10. Platzack (2004) notes that the presence of *som* in questions like this is fully acceptable only when the preceding *wh*-phrase is D-linked, for reasons that escape me.

11. Kayne's (1995) proposals on relative clause structure are largely compatible with my analysis here, given certain obvious modifications.

12. The structure of clauses in which *qui* is used to allow long *wh*-movement of a subject is clarified in section 4.5.

13. I differ from Chomsky (1986a), who finds some slight effect even here.

14. Speaker variation on the acceptability of verb-second in relative clauses certainly exists, however, as the (i) judgment indicates.

(i) *Icelandic* (Schwartz and Vikner 1996, attrib. to Thráinsson, p.c.)
    *Helgi hefur keypt   bók, sem trúlega   hefur Jón ekki lesið
    Helgi has   bought book   probably has Jón not read

15. The data examined by Vikner (1991) leads him to conclude that Icelandic does not pattern with Yiddish (and English), and that verb-second clauses are islands in Icelandic. I am assuming that Rögnvaldsson's judgments are more representative of the situation for Icelandic generally, although further work is clearly necessary to clarify the situation.

The fact that there is disagreement on the status of crucial examples is itself significant, because it indicates that the principles that interfere with extraction from this type of clause in symmetric languages are not the same as the strong constraint blocking such movement in German or Swedish. In the asymmetric languages, there is no disagreement on the existence of verb-second islands, which are responsible for sharp judgments of ungrammaticality. In contrast, if the (76) examples are less than fully grammatical for some speakers, they are still apparently less objectionable than their Dutch or Danish counterparts.

16. Vikner (1991) contains the most thorough examination of how the different Germanic languages vary in this respect.

Bentzen et al. (2007) compare several Scandinavian languages and conclude that embedded verb-second complements require a matrix verb that is "strongly or weakly asserted" or "semifactive." Heycock (2006) discusses a slightly larger set of contexts that license embedded verb-second word order, including extent clauses.

17. Exceptionally, the complementizer in asymmetric coordination is Force rather than Force*, because it does provoke a Fin goal.

18. Pesetsky (1998) proposes that overt complementizers must appear at the left edge of their clause at PF.

19. Noonan (1996) develops an account of German verb-second clauses in which movement much like that in (86) takes place. In German, there is no visible complementizer in verb-second clauses, so it cannot be determined from the word order if anything has raised to a pre-Force position. Noonan's approach evidently cannot generalize to languages of the Dutch or Swedish type.

20. Müller (1995) replicates Zwart's argument that verb-second islands cannot be equated with wh-islands. He provides the contrasting data in (i) and (ii).

(i) *Radios glaube ich gestern   hat Fritz repariert.
    radios believe I yesterday has Fritz fixed

(ii) ??Radios weiß ich nicht wie (daß) man repariert.
     radios know I   not how that one fixes

21. As Rizzi and Shlonsky further observe, wh-movement or focus movement of the locative PP is also compatible with the generation of a locative inversion structure. For my purposes, what is critical is simply that some Ā head in the left periphery be present to compel movement of the PP.

22. Rizzi and Shlonsky also maintain that the preposed locative raises first to [Spec, Fin] before being attracted to [Spec, Top] or [Spec, Foc]. Their justification for this movement has to do with the special way that their "Subject Criterion" is satisfied in locative inversion structures. In the analysis developed here, locative

movement to [Spec, Fin] results from the same principles that drive subjects to [Spec, Fin] generally.

23. The presence of a [FORCE] feature in topics might provide a motivation for preferring the variant theory suggested in note 5. In that case, the [FORCE] feature would be a property of null operators that will be associated with sentential topics. Topics themselves would never need to bear [FORCE].

24. Bošković and Lasnik attribute the basic idea to Pesetsky (1992), who proposes that null C incorporates into the matrix verb. For my purposes, it is important that the operation licensing English null Force is not true syntactic incorporation, because ForceP should be expected to become an extraction island if Force is incorporated. But Bošković and Lasnik's notion of morphological merger does not imply that Force cannot attract specifiers, so no island effects are expected.

25. An anonymous referee suggests that French "pseudo-relative" structures like (i) may be problematic if *qui* must appear at the edge of their clause.

(i) J'ai   vu   Marie qui courait.
    I-have seen Marie   was-running
    'I saw Marie run.'

And indeed, such examples are not explained by my approach. In fact, to my knowledge, they are not fully explained by any approach in the existing literature. (Important partial analyses of this construction include Burzio 1986 and Guasti 1993.) As such, they must be regarded less as counterexamples than as problems where further research is needed.

26. In previous accounts of the *que-qui* alternation, such as Taraldsen 1986a and Rizzi 1990a, special mechanisms have had to be invented to ensure that *qui* appears only when the subject is extracted. Nothing extra is necessary in the present model, because the fact that subjects are raised to [Spec, Fin] is already ensured by the P-feature of Fin.

27. Rizzi and Shlonsky (2007) also conclude that successful subject extraction is from [Spec, Fin], with *qui* = Fin. For them, however, the subject occupies [Spec, Fin] only when subject extraction occurs, much as in the analysis of Pesetsky and Torrego 2000. Since I have argued that subjects will normally occupy the [Spec, Fin] position, the analysis must be substantially different.

28. To be consistent with the Bošković and Lasnik model, we would assume that the null Fin is not required to undergo Morphological Merger, because that licensing condition holds only of the regular null declarative C. English Fin can stand on its own. No problem arises therefore when the matrix verb and FinP are not adjacent.

29. The terminology, again, is from Pesetsky 1992.

30. Henry (1992) shows that Belfast English allows *for* to appear to the right of the subject in complements to *want*-class verbs.

(i) I wanted Jimmy for to come with me.

(ii) I don't like the children for to be out late.

In this dialect, evidently, *for* may appear either in Fin or in Force. *For* only assigns Case when it appears in the latter position, though.

31. The initial empirical observation is due to Bresnan 1976; obviously her characterization of the structural context was different.

Chapter 5

1. See Bouchard 1984 for discussion of this general point, in the context of a theory of empty categories.

2. An anonymous reviewer correctly points out that we might expect some variation in speaker judgments for sentences like (27a), since some speakers appear to accept bare FinP complements as indirect questions, as discussed in section 4.3. With *if* functioning as a force marker, the problematic operator to its left should then be ignored at the LF interface. To the best of my knowledge, however, no speakers accept subject extraction from an *if*-clause. One difference between this type of complement clause and its declarative counterpart is that the *if* and the operator to its left are both signifiers of interrogative force. It may be that the CEIC is only operative when there are two distinct types of force markers appearing at the edge of the clause.

3. In example (47), the verb movement itself will not be motivated, and the word order would therefore be different, if there is no Top head present to block incorporation of Fin by C.

4. Extraction from a clause with the *som* complementizer is also barred, as example (i) from Platzack 1986 shows, but this cannot be assumed to be a *that*-trace effect.

(i) *Vilken film kunde ingen   minnas   [vem (som) alla   trodde [som
    which film could no-one remember   who (that) everyone thought   that
    hade regisserat?
    had   directed

The problem with (i) is that *som* is used as a force marker for a declarative clause, when it can only signify relative clause force.

5. There may be a connection, as well, with the relationship between matrix negators and the possibility of embedded verb-second complements discussed in Reinholtz 1993. Matrix negators make embedded verb-second complements impossible. Reinholtz maintains that complementizers with a negative feature must be selected in negative polarity contexts (Laka 1990), and that such complementizers are incompatible with verb-second structure. In the model developed here, such negative complementizers would not be susceptible to incorporation—abstract or overt—by the matrix verb.

6. As for the improvement that appears with an auxiliary verb in the complement clause, I am at a loss.

7. The Scandinavian data in (51)–(53) is important because it shows quite clearly how irrelevant any notion of government—antecedent or lexical—is to

the *that*-trace effect. If we imagine that the subject trace is in Spec-TP, then every form of government from outside TP will be blocked in sentences like (53), since lexical government cannot access anything inside CP, and since antecedent government must always be blocked by the *wh*-phrase *hva*. The alternative proposed here relies only on the content of the set of features borne by Fin, which may vary according to the context (and the language).

8. I am grateful to Alison Henry for generously finding this data for me.

9. Vikner (1991) expressly attributes the unacceptability of this type of sentence to the ECP.

References

Åfarli, T. 1986. Absence of V2 effects in a dialect of Norwegian. In O. Dahl and A. Holmberg, eds., *Scandinavian Syntax: Workshop at the Ninth Scandinavian Conference of Linguistics*, 8–20. Stockholm: Stockholms universitet, Institut för lingvistik.

Allen, B. J., D. B. Gardiner, and D. G. Frantz. 1984. Noun incorporation in Southern Tiwa. *International Journal of American Linguistics* 50(3), 292–311.

Anderson, S. R. 1993. Wackernagel's revenge: Clitics, morphology and the syntax of second position. *Language* 69, 68–98.

Andrews, A. 1982. Case in modern Icelandic. In J. Bresnan, ed., *The Mental Representation of Grammatical Relations*. Cambridge, MA: MIT Press.

Baker, M. 1988. *Incorporation: A Theory of Grammatical Function Changing*. Chicago: University of Chicago Press.

Bayer, J. 1984. COMP in Bavarian syntax. *Linguistic Review* 3(3), 209–274.

Bayer, J., and E. Brandner. 2008. On wh-head-movement and the Doubly-Filled-Comp filter. In C. B. Chang and H. J. Haynie, eds., *Proceedings of the 26th West Coast Conference on Formal Linguistics*, 87–95. Somerville, MA: Cascadilla Proceedings Project.

Belletti, A. 1990. *Generalized Verb Movement: Aspects of Verb Syntax*. Torino: Rosenberg and Sellier.

Bennis, H., and L. Haegeman. 1984. On the status of agreement and relative clauses in West Flemish. In W. de Geest and Y. Putseys, eds., *Sentential Complementation*, 33–53. Dordrecht: Foris.

Bentzen, K., T. Hróarsdóttir, G. H. Hrafnbjargarson, and A.-L. Wiklund. 2007, January. Embedded V2 in Scandinavian: Empirical observations. Unpublished handout from NORMS workshop on Verb Movement, Reykjavík, January 26, 2007.

Bobaljik, J., and P. Branigan. 2006. Eccentric agreement and multiple case-checking. In A. Johns, D. Massam, and J. Ndirayagije, eds., *Ergativity*. Dordrecht: Springer.

Bonet, E. 1991. *Morphology after Syntax*. Doctoral dissertation, MIT.

Bošković, Ž. 1997. *The Syntax of Nonfinite Complementation: An Economy Approach.* Cambridge, MA: MIT Press.

Bošković, Ž. 1999. On multiple feature checking: Multiple *Wh*-fronting and multiple head movement. In S. D. Epstein and N. Hornstein, eds., *Working Minimalism*, 159–187. Cambridge, MA: MIT Press.

Bošković, Ž., and H. Lasnik. 2003. On the distribution of null complementizers. *Linguistic Inquiry* 34(4), 527–546.

Bouchard, D. 1984. *On the Content of Empty Categories.* Dordrecht: Foris.

Bouchard, D., and P. Hirschbühler. 1986. French quoi and its clitic allomorph que. In C. Neidle and R. N. Cedeño, eds., *Studies in Romance Languages*, 39–60. Dordrecht: Foris.

Branigan, P. 1992. *Subjects and Complementizers.* Doctoral dissertation, MIT. Distributed by MIT Working Papers in Linguistics.

Branigan, P. 1996a. Treating *that*-trace variation. In J. Black and V. Motapanyane, eds., *Microparametric Syntax: Dialect Variation in Syntax*, 25–39. Amsterdam: John Benjamins.

Branigan, P. 1996b. Verb-second and the A-bar syntax of subjects. *Studia Linguistica* 50(1), 51–79.

Branigan, P., and C. Collins. 1993. Verb movement and the quotative construction in English. *MIT Working Papers in Linguistics* 18, 1–13.

Branigan, P., and M. MacKenzie. 2002. Altruism, A-bar movement and object agreement in Innu-aimûn. *Linguistic Inquiry* 33(3), 385–407.

Bresnan, J. 1976. Variables in the theory of transformations. In P. Culicover, T. Wasow, and A. Akmajian, eds., *Formal Syntax*, 157–196. Academic Press.

Bresnan, J. 1994. Locative inversion and the architecture of Universal Grammar. *Language* 70(1), 72–131.

Burzio, L. 1986. *Italian Syntax.* Studies in Natural Language and Linguistic Theory. Dordrecht: Reidel.

Chomsky, N. 1955/1975. *Logical Structure of Linguistic Theory.* New York: Plenum. Excerpted from unpublished 1955/1956 manuscript.

Chomsky, N. 1957. *Syntactic Structures.* The Hague: Mouton.

Chomsky, N. 1977. On wh-movement. In T. W. P. Culicover and A. Akmajian, eds., *Formal Syntax.* New York: Academic Press.

Chomsky, N. 1981. *Lectures on Government and Binding.* Dordrecht: Foris.

Chomsky, N. 1982. *Concepts and Consequences of the Theory of Government and Binding.* Cambridge, MA: MIT Press.

Chomsky, N. 1986a. *Barriers.* Cambridge, MA: MIT Press.

Chomsky, N. 1986b. *Knowledge of Language: Its Nature, Origin, and Use.* New York: Praeger.

Chomsky, N. 1993. A Minimalist Program for linguistic theory. In K. Hale and S. J. Keyser, eds., *The View from Building 20: Essays in Linguistics in Honor of Sylvain Bromberger*, 1–52. Cambridge, MA: MIT Press.

Chomsky, N. 1995. *The Minimalist Program.* Cambridge, MA: MIT Press.

Chomsky, N. 2000. Minimalist inquiries: The framework. In R. Martin, D. Michaels, and J. Uriagareka, eds., *Step by Step: Essays on Minimalist Syntax in Honor of Howard Lasnik.* Cambridge, MA: MIT Press.

Chomsky, N. 2001. Derivation by phase. In M. Kenstowicz, ed., *Ken Hale: A Life in Language.* Cambridge, MA: MIT Press.

Chomsky, N. 2004. Beyond explanatory accuracy. In A. Belletti, ed., *Structures and Beyond: The Cartography of Syntactic Structures*, vol. 3, 104–191. Oxford: Oxford University Press.

Chomsky, N. 2007. Approaching UG from below. Unpublished ms., MIT.

Chomsky, N. 2008. On phases. In R. Freidin, C. P. Otero, and M. L. Zubizarreta, eds., *Foundational Issues in Linguistic Theory Essays in Honor of Jean-Roger Vergnaud.* Cambridge, MA: MIT Press.

Chomsky, N., and H. Lasnik. 1977. Filters and control. *Linguistic Inquiry* 8, 425–504.

Chung, S., and J. McCloskey. 1983. On the interpretation of certain island facts in GPSG. *Linguistic Inquiry* 14, 704–713.

Cole, P., and G. Hermon. 1998. The typology of wh-movement: Wh- questions in Malay. *Syntax* 1(3), 221–258.

Collins, C. 1996. *Local Economy.* Cambridge, MA: MIT Press.

Collins, C. 2002. Multiple verb movement in †Hoan. *Linguistic Inquiry* 33(1), 1–29.

Collins, C., and P. Branigan. 1997. Quotative Inversion. *Natural Language and Linguistic Theory* 15, 1–41.

Culicover, P. 1991. Topicalization, inversion, and complementizers in English. Ms., Ohio State University.

Culicover, P. 1993. The adverb effect: Evidence against ECP accounts of that-t effects. *NELS* 24, 97–110.

Dayal, V. 1994. Scope marking as indirect wh-dependency. *Natural Language Semantics* 2, 137–170.

DeHaan, G., and F. Weerman. 1986. Finiteness and verb fronting in Frisian. In H. Haider and M. Prinzhorn, eds., *Verb Second Phenomena in Germanic Languages*, 77–110. Dordrecht: Foris.

Den Besten, H. 1983. On the interaction of root transformations and lexical deletive rules. In W. Abraham, ed., *On the Formal Syntax of the Westgermania*, 47–131. Amsterdam: John Benjamins.

Diesing, M. 1990. Verb movement and the subject position in Yiddish. *Natural Language and Linguistic Theory* 8, 41–79.

Dikken, M. D., and A. Næss. 1993. Case dependencies: The case of predicate inversion. *Linguistic Review* 10, 303–336.

Engdahl, E. 1984. *The Syntax and Semantics of Constituent Questions with Special Reference to Swedish.* Dordrecht: Reidel.

Epstein, S. D., and T. D. Seely. 2006. *Derivations in Minimalism.* Cambridge: Cambridge University Press.

Fanselow, G. 2006. Partial movement. In M. Everaert, H. van Riemsdijk, R. Goedemans, and B. Hollebrandse, eds., *The Blackwell Companion to Syntax.* London: Blackwell.

Fitzpatrick, J. 2006. Deletion through movement. *Natural Language and Linguistic Theory* 24(2), 399–431.

Frampton, J., and S. Gutmann. 2000. Agreement is feature sharing. Unpublished ms., Northeastern University.

Goeman, T. 1980. COMP-agreement? In W. Zonneveld and F. Weerman, eds., *Linguistics in the Netherlands 1977–1979*, 291–306. Dordrecht: Foris.

Groenendijk, J., and M. Stokhof. 1984. Semantic analysis of wh-complements. *Linguistics and Philosophy* 5, 77–164.

Guasti, T. 1993. *Causative and Perception Verbs.* Turin: Rosenberg and Selier.

Gueron, J., and T. Hoekstra. 1988. T-chains and the constituent structure of auxiliaries.

Haegeman, L. 2003. Notes on long adverbial fronting in English and the left periphery. *Linguistic Inquiry* 34(4), 640–649.

Haider, H. 1984. Topic, focus, and V-second. *Groninger Arbeiten zur Germanistischen Linguistik* 25, 72–120.

Haider, H. 1989. *Parameter der deutschen Syntax.* Tübingen: Narr.

Hale, K., and S. J. Keyser. 1993. On argument structure and the lexical expression of syntactic relations. In K. Hale and S. J. Keyser, eds., *The View from Building 20: Essays in Honor of Sylvain Bromberger*, 53–110. Cambridge, MA: MIT Press.

Halle, M., and A. Marantz. 1993. Distributed morphology and the pieces of inflection. In K. Hale and S. J. Keyser, eds., *The View from Building 20: Essays in Honor of Sylvain Bromberger*, 111–176. Cambridge, MA: MIT Press.

Hellan, L., and K. K. Christensen, eds. 1986. *Topics in Scandinavian Syntax.* Dordrecht: Reidel.

Henry, A. 1992. Infinitives in a for-to dialect. *Natural Language and Linguistic Theory* 10(2), 233–277.

Henry, A. 1995. *Belfast English and Standard English.* Oxford: Oxford University Press.

Heycock, C. 2006. Embedded root phenomena. In M. Everaert and H. van Riemsdijk, eds., *The Blackwell Companion to Syntax*, vol. 2, 174–209. Oxford: Blackwell.

Hiraiwa, K. 2005. *Dimensions of Symmetries in Syntax: Agreement and Clausal Architecture.* Doctoral dissertation, MIT.

Hoekstra, E. 1994. Expletive replacement, verb-second and coordination. *Linguistic Review* 11, 285–297.

Hoekstra, T., and H. Bennis. 1989. Why Kaatje was not heard sing a song. In D. Jaspers, W. Kloosters, Y. Putseys, and P. Seuren, eds., *Sentential Complementation and the Lexicon*, 21–40. Dordrecht: Foris.

Holmberg, A. 1986. *Word Order and Syntactic Features.* Doctoral dissertation, University of Stockholm.

Holmberg, A. 2000. Scandinavian stylistic fronting: How any category can become an expletive. *Linguistic Inquiry* 31, 445–483.

Holmberg, A., and C. Platzack. 2005. The Scandinavian languages. In G. Cinque and R. Kayne, eds., *The Oxford Handbook of Comparative Syntax*, 420–458. Oxford: Oxford University Press.

Johns, A. 2000. Movement and languages with complex morphology. *University of Maryland Working Papers in Linguistics* 10, 113–125.

Kayne, R. S. 1972. French relative "que." In F. Hensey and M. Luján, eds., *Current Studies in Romance Linguistics*, 255–299. Washington, DC: Georgetown University Press.

Kayne, R. S. 1975. *French Syntax: The Transformational Cycle.* Cambridge, MA: MIT Press.

Kayne, R. S. 1984. *Connectedness and Binary Branching.* Dordrecht: Foris.

Kayne, R. S. 1989a. Facets of past participle agreement in Romance. In P. Beninca, ed., *Dialect Variation in the Theory of Grammar.* Dordrecht: Foris.

Kayne, R. S. 1989b. Notes on English agreement. *CIEFL Bulletin* 1, 41–67.

Kayne, R. S. 1995. *The Antisymmetry of Syntax.* Cambridge, MA: MIT Press.

Kayne, R. S., and J.-Y. Pollock. 2001. New thoughts on stylistic inversion. In A. Hulk and J.-Y. Pollock, eds., *Subject Inversion in Romance and the Theory of Universal Grammar*, 107–162. Oxford: Oxford University Press.

Kim, K.-S. 2008. English C moves downward as well as upward: An extension of Bošković and Lasnik's (2003) approach. *Linguistic Inquiry* 39(2), 295–307.

Koster, J. 1978. Why subject sentences don't exist. In S. J. Keyser, ed., *Recent Transformational Studies in European Languages*, 53–64. Cambridge, MA: MIT Press.

Koster, J. 1987. *Domains and Dynasties.* Dordrecht: Foris.

Krapova, I., and G. Cinque. 2008. On the order of wh-phrases in Bulgarian multiple wh-fronting. In G. Zybatow, et al., ed., *Formal Description of Slavic Languages: The Fifth Conference, Leipzig 2003*, Linguistik International, 318–336. Frankfurt am Main: Peter Lang.

Laka, I. 1990. *Negation in Syntax: On the Nature of Functional Categories and Projections.* Doctoral dissertation, MIT.

Larson, R. K. 1985. On the syntax of disjunction scope. *Natural Language and Linguistic Theory* 3, 217–264.

Lasnik, H. 2003. On the Extended Projection Principle. *Studies in Modern Grammar* 31, 1–23.

Lasnik, H., and M. Saito. 1992. *Affect-α.* Cambridge, MA: MIT Press.

Linebarger, M. 1980. *The Grammar of Negative Polarity.* Doctoral dissertation, MIT.

Maling, J., and A. Zaenan. 1978. The nonuniversality of a surface filter. *Linguistic Inquiry* 9(3), 475–498.

May, R. 1977. *The Grammar of Quantification.* Doctoral dissertation, MIT.

McCloskey, J. 2007. Questions and questioning in a local English. Ms., UC Santa Cruz.

McDaniel, D. 1989. Partial and multiple Wh-movement. *Natural Language and Linguistic Theory* 7(4), 565–604.

Meer, G. V. D. 1988. Reported speech and the position of the finite verb (some facts from West Frisian). *Leuvense Bijdragen* 77, 301–324.

Moorcroft, R. 1995. *Clause-Level Functional Categories in Germanic V2 Languages.* Doctoral dissertation, University of Toronto.

Müller, G. 1995. *A-Bar Syntax: A Study in Movement Types.* Berlin: Mouton de Gruyter.

Müller, G. 1997. Partial wh-movement and optimality theory. *Linguistic Review* 14, 249–306.

Noonan, M. 1996. Functional architecture and wh-movement. Ms., Université du Québec à Montréal.

Nunes, J. 2004. *Linearization of Chains and Sideward Movement.* Vol. 43. Cambridge, MA: MIT Press.

Pesetsky, D. 1982. Complementizer trace phenomena and the nominative island condition. *Linguistic Review* 1, 297–343.

Pesetsky, D. 1992. Zero syntax. Vol. 2. Ms., MIT.

Pesetsky, D. 1994. Some long-lost relatives of Burzio's generalization. Paper presented at the conference on Burzio's Generalization, the Netherlands.

Pesetsky, D. 1998. Optimality principles of sentence pronounciation. In P. Barbosa, D. Fox, P. Hagstrom, M. McGinnis, and D. Pesetsky, eds., *Is the Best Good Enough? Optimality and Competition in Syntax.* Cambridge, MA: MIT Press.

Pesetsky, D. 2000. *Phrasal Movement and Its Kin.* Cambridge, MA: MIT Press.

Pesetsky, D., and E. Torrego. 2000. T-to-C movement: Causes and consequences. In M. Kenstowicz, ed., *Ken Hale: A Life in Language.* Cambridge, MA: MIT Press.

Pesetsky, D., and E. Torrego. 2007. The syntax of valuation and the interpretability of features. In S. Karimi, V. Samiian, and W. Wilkins, eds., *Phrasal and Clausal Architecture: Syntactic Derivation and Interpretation.* Amsterdam: Benjamins.

Platzack, C. 1986. COMP, INFL, and Germanic word order. In L. Hellan and K. K. Christensen, eds., *Topics in Scandinavian Syntax*, 185–234. Studies in Natural Language and Linguistic Theory. Dordrecht: Reidel.

Platzack, C. 2004. Cross-linguistic word order variation at the left periphery: The case of object first main clauses. In D. Adger, C. D. Cat, and G. Tsoulas, eds., *Peripheries: Syntactic Edges and Their Effects*, 191–210. New York: Springer.

Poletto, C., and J.-Y. Pollock. 2004. On wh-clitics and wh-doubling in French and some North Eastern Italian dialects. *Probus* 16(2), 241–272.

Polinsky, M., and E. Potsdam. 2001. The syntax of topic and long-distance agreement in Tsez. *Natural Language and Linguistic Theory* 19, 583–646.

Progovac, L. 1992. Nonnegative polarity licensing must involve Comp. *Linguistic Inquiry* 23, 341–347.

Reinholtz, C. 1993. Verb second, negation, and minimality in Danish. In J. Mead, ed., *Proceedings of the Eleventh West Coast Conference on Formal Linguistics (WCCFL-11)*, 405–420. Stanford, CA: CSLI.

Rice, C., and P. Svenonius. 1998. Prosodic V2 in Northern Norwegian. Ms., University of Tromso.

Richards, N. 1997. *What Moves Where in Which Language?* Doctoral dissertation, MIT.

Richards, N. 1998. The principle of Minimal Compliance. *Linguistic Inquiry* 29, 599–629.

Rizzi, L. 1990a. *Relativized Minimality*. Cambridge, MA: MIT Press.

Rizzi, L. 1990b. Speculations on verb second. In J. Mascaró and M. Nespor, eds., *Grammar in Progress: Glow Essays for Henk van Riemsdijk*, 375–386. Dordrecht: Foris.

Rizzi, L. 1996. Residual verb second and the *Wh*-criterion. In A. Belletti and L. Rizzi, eds., *Parameters and Functional Heads: Essays in Comparative Syntax*, 63–90. Oxford: Oxford University Press.

Rizzi, L. 1997. The fine structure of the left periphery. In L. Haegeman, ed., *Elements of Grammar*. Dordrecht: Kluwer.

Rizzi, L. 1999, January. On the position "int(errogative)" in the left periphery of the clause. Ms., Università di Siena.

Rizzi, L. 2003. On the form of chains: Criterial positions and the ECP. In L. L. Cheng and N. Corver, eds., *On Wh Movement*. Cambridge, MA: MIT Press.

Rizzi, L. 2004. Locality and the left periphery. In A. Belletti, ed., *Structures and Beyond: The Cartography of Syntactic Structures*, vol. 3, 223–251. Oxford: Oxford University Press.

Rizzi, L., and U. Shlonsky. 2006. Satisfying the subject criterion by a non subject: English locative inversion and heavy NP shift. In M. Frascarelli, ed., *Phases of Interpretation*, 341–361. Berlin: Mouton de Gruyter.

Rizzi, L., and U. Shlonsky. 2007. Strategies of subject extraction. In H. M. Gärtner and U. Sauerland, eds., *Interfaces + Recursion = Language? Chomsky's Minimalism and the View from Syntax-Semantics*, 115–160. Berlin: Mouton de Gruyter.

Roberts, I. 2001. Head movement. In M. Baltin and C. Collins, eds., *The Handbook of Contemporary Syntactic Theory*, 113–147. Oxford: Blackwell.

Roberts, I., and A. Roussou. 1998. The Extended Projection Principle as a condition on the Tense-dependency. Unpublished ms., University of Stuttgart and University of Wales, Bangor.

Rögnvaldsson, E. 1984. Icelandic word order and það-insertion. *Working Papers in Scandinavian Syntax* 8, 1–21.

Ross, R. 1967. *Island Constraints in Syntax.* Doctoral dissertation, MIT.

Rothstein, S. 1983. *The Syntactic Forms of Predication.* Doctoral dissertation, MIT.

Rudin, C. 1988. On multiple questions and multiple WH fronting. *Natural Language and Linguistic Theory* 6, 445–501.

Ruwet, N. 1972. *Théorie syntaxique et syntaxe du français.* Paris: Seuil.

Salzmann, M. 2005. On an alternative to long A′-movement in German and Dutch. *Leiden Papers in Linguistics* 2(3), 107–128.

Schwartz, B., and S. Vikner. 1989. All verb second clauses are CPs. *Working Papers in Scandinavian Syntax* 43, 27–49.

Schwartz, B., and S. Vikner. 1996. The verb always leaves IP in V2 clauses. In A. Belletti and L. Rizzi, eds., *Parameters and Functional Heads: Essays in Comparative Syntax*, 11–62. Oxford: Oxford University Press.

Shlonsky, U. 1994. Agreement in Comp. *Linguistic Review* 11, 351–375.

Sigurdhsson, H. 1997. Stylistic fronting. Ms., University of Iceland.

Sobin, N. 1987. The variable status of COMP-trace phenomena. *Natural Language and Linguistic Theory* 5, 33–60.

Staudacher, P. 1990. Long movement from verb-second-complements in German. In G. Grewendorf and W. Sternefeld, eds., *Scrambling and Barriers*, 319–339. Amsterdam: Benjamins.

Stowell, T. 1981. *Origins of Phrase Structure.* Doctoral dissertation, MIT.

Suñer, M. 2000. The syntax of direct quotes with special reference to Spanish and English. *Natural Language and Linguistic Theory* 18(3), 525–578.

Taraldsen, T. 1986a. *Som* and the binding theory. In L. Hellan and K. K. Christensen, eds., *Topics in Scandinavian Syntax*, 149–184. Dordrecht: Reidel.

Taraldsen, T. 1986b. On verb second and the functional content of syntactic categories. In H. Haider and M. Prinzhorn, eds., *Verb Second Phenomena in Germanic Languages*, 7–25. Dordrecht: Foris.

Thrainsson, H. 1986. V1, V2, V3 in Icelandic. In H. Haider and M. Prinzhorn, eds., *Verb-Second Phenomena in the Germanic Languages.* Dordrecht: Foris.

Travis, L. 1984. *Parameters and Effects of Word Order Variation.* Doctoral dissertation, MIT.

Ura, H. 2000. *Checking Theory and Grammatical Relations in Universal Grammar.* Oxford: Oxford University Press.

Van Craenenbroeck, J., and M. van Koppen. 2002, April. The locality of agreement and the CP-domain. Talk handout. GLOW 25, Amsterdam.

Van Koppen, M. 2005. *One Probe—Two Goals: Aspects of Agreement in Dutch Dialects.* Doctoral dissertation, University of Leiden. LOT-Publications 105. http://www.lotpublications.nl/publish/articles/001227/bookpart.pdf.

Vikner, S. 1991. *Verb Movement and the Licensing of NP-Positions in the Germanic Languages.* Doctoral dissertation, Université de Genève.

Wechsler, S. 1991. Verb second and illocutionary force. In K. Leffel and D. Bouchard, eds., *Views on Phrase Structure*, 177–191. Dordrecht: Kluwer Academic Publishers.

Williams, E. 1978. Across-the-board extraction. *Linguistic Inquiry* 9, 31–42.

Wolfart, H. C. 1971. Plains Cree internal syntax and the problem of noun incorporation. In *Proceedings of the Thirty-Eighth International Congress of Americanists*, vol. 3, 511–518.

Wolfart, H. C. 1973. *Plains Cree: A Grammatical Study.* Transactions of the American Philosophical Society, New Series 63, part 5. American Philosophical Society.

Wolfart, H. C. 2008, February. Syntactic relations within and beyond the noun. Talk at UBC Cree Linguistics Workshop.

Zwart, C. J.-W. 1993. Verb agreement and complementizer agreement. *MIT Working Papers in Linguistics* 18, 297–340.

Zwart, C. J.-W. 1997. *Morphosyntax of Verb Movement: A Minimalist Approach to the Syntax of Dutch.* Dordrecht: Kluwer.

Zwart, C. J.-W. 2001. Syntactic and phonological verb movement. *Syntax* 4(1), 34–62.

Index

Linguistic Inquiry Monographs

Samuel Jay Keyser, general editor